This is How We Hewitt

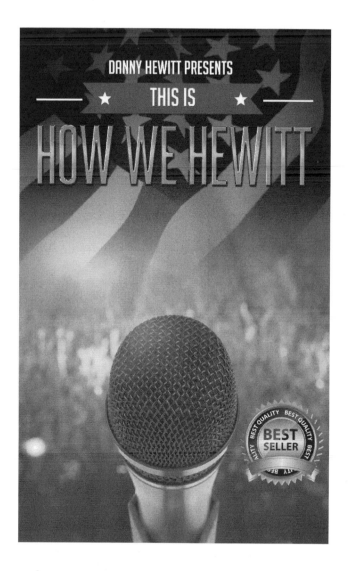

Table of Content

Acknowledgements

Writing this book has been such a long and enduring struggle for me. When I was in 11th grade English, I failed during the regular school year and had to take it again in summer school just to graduate on time. When I made it to the 12th grade, my teacher told me that I would either end up in jail or as the President of the United States. When I finally took the SATs, I got 650 in math and 500 in English. To say the least, English has never been my strong suit. Anyone who has ever attempted to write a book would understand this was not an easy process. You don't just jot some things down, and then, BAM, you have a book. It has taken me days, weeks, months, and even years to get through this first book of mine. I learned once again that obstacles will get in your way in life, but if you continue to get up when knocked down, you too can achieve something great.

Several people in my life have pushed me to write this book for my kids, my family, and of course myself. My grandmother, who thinks I am her favorite, will be so proud of me, but little does she know that I am super proud of her. She was married at a very young age and raised five children selflessly. Her inspiration and positive attitude have always helped me be an optimistic person in this world. She has enabled me to focus on the positive things in life and avoid the negative. Thank you for always be the sunshine in my life grandma. I love you! You inspire me!

My parents, my mom and my dad, are in many ways the reason I am who I am today. My father, a fierce competitor in *everything* he does, taught me my fanatical drive to win and how second place is never good enough. He taught me how you would die if you stop growing in life. Time and time again, my father has not allowed me to take the easy road in life but driven me to find greatness in pursuing a larger and more meaningful path each and every day God allows me to wake up. My mother, a firecracker in her own way, taught me how hard work is a necessity in life. She didn't let me sleep in late, skip my homework, or avoid practice. Instead, she taught me that you must work hard every day if you want to achieve greatness and want to win. I love you, mom and dad, for making me the man I am today! When times get tough, I think about many of the life lessons I have learned from each of you, and it gives me the confidence to keep going. Mom and dad, you inspire me!

Several great friends of mine truly wouldn't leave me alone about writing a book. Michael Debenham, CEO of American Title Loans, has been pushing me to write a book for probably five or six years now. Mike is one of the greatest friends in my life. He has truly shown me what being a friend is all about. Thank you for never giving up on me, Mike.

Mike is a true underdog going against the big dogs. Watch out for American Title Loans. They are practicing and preparing to win. I am betting on Mike.

Chad Corman: co-writer, ghostwriter, editor, coach, and teammate, has continued to drive me to finish this book. Without you, Chad, this would still be on a white board in our conference room as a dream. You have believed in me throughout the entire process, and I am forever grateful for all of the time, energy, and enthusiasm you have put into this first book of mine. Thanks for showing me how *you* Hewitt.

I want to say a special thanks to one of my mentors and one of the most inspirational persons I have known in my life, Gordon D'Angelo. Your unstoppable optimism has been a guide for me and so many others. You truly are one of a kind. Thanks for pushing me to get this book completed. You showed me that if you create a *vision* and put the proper preparation in, you can do anything you want in this world.

I could thank dozens, if not hundreds, of others for their time and commitment to investing in my life, but that would be a book in itself. Thank you to everyone who has believed in me and pushed me to become who I am today. I will see you at the top!

Preface

The most simple definition of an "underdog" is a person, group, or team who is expected to lose. On the flip side, the individual, group, or team who is expected to win is known as the "favorite" or "top dog." In the case where an underdog wins, the outcome is an "upset." These terms are commonly used in sports betting and politics. However, the term is believed first to have been used in the blood sport known as bear-baiting, where the "top-dog" was trained to attack the bear's head and throat, and the "underdog" was trained to attack the bear's underside. The top-dog had a better chance of surviving and beating the bear, whereas the underdog was more likely to lose and die – almost invariably! This is a book about being an underdog and not only surviving but *winning!* Winning when all the odds are against you! When everyone *believes* there is *no way you could win*!

H&R Block, Jackson Hewitt, and Liberty Tax are the three largest tax preparation companies that have ever existed. While these industry giants currently enjoy being the "top-dogs" of an industry that consists of nearly forty thousand companies employing over 130,000 people that serve nearly 150 million individuals and 2.4 million corporations, none of them started out at the top with a guarantee that they would collect their current piece of the eight plus billion-dollar industry in future years. Aside from taxes and climbing from the bottom to the top, they all have one thing in common – my father and I. This book tells their story, our story, my story. It is a story about underdogs and, most importantly, a story for underdogs.

Are you an underdog? Have you ever been an underdog? Do you know what it feels like to have *everyone betting against you*? Only you who are reading this book knows the true answer to that question, but it's a safe bet that most of you, like me, are underdogs. I believe each of us is an underdog most of the time of our life. God didn't put you on this earth to make it easy for you. You have to work hard and overcome obstacle after obstacle to achieve greatness in this tough world we live in.

I have realized later in life that I was raised in an environment that could influence any run-of-the-mill, normal, everyday "underdog" to make it their mission to shred through any obstacles that stood in the way of realizing the status of "top-dog." We trained. We practiced. We worked. We got knocked down, *but we got up*! You have to get up! You don't have a choice. Life will give you obstacle after obstacle to overcome. It is how we react to these obstacles that determine our fate in life.

No matter what you set out to do, whether you want to become an entrepreneur, a professional athlete, apply for a new job or whatever it is, many of us feel like an underdog in life. Many of us feel like we don't understand how we can compete. How can we compete against these big companies, big government, or against these people that are taller, stronger, faster and better than us? How are we going to survive in the playing field against the person, the company, the people, or the business that has everything going for them? It looks like everything is going against us. It looks as if the "top-dog" will win hands down. Will we get knocked down? All of us get knocked down! All of us have struggles and tribulations. Getting knocked down is *inevitable.* Getting back up is not. It is a choice we get to make each and every moment of our life. Do we win the day?

In this book, I will share with you the ups and downs that my family has gone through in our years in the tax business. I will share with you obstacle after obstacle that has stood in our way, and I will show you how even when things got tough, underdogs *always stand back up*! From reading it, I hope you will learn how to compete when all the odds are against you. I hope you will understand what it takes to win as an underdog. You will hear stories from real life underdogs trying to survive in this world. If you have ever felt like an underdog, betted on an underdog, or just all around love underdogs like I do, then this book is for you. I want to help you win as an underdog.

Chapter 1
A New Underdog Cometh...

My family has worked with, owned, developed, created, and done almost everything you can imagine in all the three major income tax brands, H&R Block, Jackson Hewitt, and Liberty Tax. But the real motivator that has driven us from the get-go is a strong sense of responsibility to help the American people.

We have to fight for every dollar we keep in this country. Most of the things that taxes cover are things that many agree on. They pay for our police officers, our firefighters, our military, our roads, public schools, public transportation, parks, and you name it. We don't disagree with the fact that we should be taxed, and we don't disagree with the fact that it should go to these great things.

However, who else do you allow in your cookie jar? Who else do you allow into your money that you want to spend? What things do you buy for yourself and your family? Where do you spend your money? It's normally where you choose and on what you want. But the reality is that for every dollar you make, the IRS comes and puts its hands on that dollar and grabs some of it from you; no matter who you are, where you live, or what you do, it wants a piece of the pie if you are American. If you earned a hundred dollars at work today, you want to know how you can keep the most of that. That is the battle that my family has been fighting for nearly fifty years! My family has helped millions of Americans complete their tax returns to save each and every one of them as much of their hard earned money as possible.

IRS debt is one of the few debts in the U.S. that can't be erased by filing for bankruptcy. You can file bankruptcy on credit cards, cars, homes, and more, but you *will* pay your IRS debt. There is no way around it. As a matter of fact, they have what they call an "offer in compromise." You would think that this offer in compromise works in such a way that if you get behind on your taxes, you can come in and get a fair deal with them. However, you are limited to only one offer in compromise in your *entire* life. If you mess up one time, and you owe forty thousand dollars to the IRS, but you don't have that money, you can offer a compromise. But you may never ask to that again. With the IRS, it's quite simply their way or the highway. Americans fear the IRS probably more than the FBI or the CIA. When you get behind with the IRS, it becomes a very real situation for many of us.

Income tax laws and the IRS are scary to most Americans for good reason. The classic example of this is the man who broke nearly every law written and still managed to elude every law enforcement agency in this country...until the IRS came to collect! While Al Capone and the majority of Americans do everything possible to avoid conflict or even contact with this agency, my parents and others, like Henry and Richard Bloch, saw this as an opportunity to help Americans everywhere to keep their money and keep the IRS out of their cookie jar. When Henry and Richard Bloch started H&R Block, their intent was to help the small business owners of America to complete, organize, and file their tax returns with the IRS. They saw a need in the United States for the average man to be represented. When they opened their doors in 1955, there was no major brand doing this yet. They were the first.

Like many businesses, H&R Block, Jackson Hewitt, and Liberty Tax open and close their books on a fiscal basis instead of a calendar year. The traditional fiscal year runs from May 1 to April 30. I was born on the dawn of the new fiscal year of 1979, May 1, 1978, to a mother and father who both worked at H&R Block. At the time, they had both been with H&R Block for more than a decade and had been integral in helping the company grow into the industry leader that we know of today. My parents had started as seasonal tax preparers and worked their way up through the ranks over the years. They first became store managers, and then they rose to be the leaders of entire regions of the country. When, on that faithful day in 1978, their "Tax Baby" arrived, I was almost immediately immersed into the world of not only taxes and finance, but also to a world of humble beginnings, exponential growth, and constant change.

In 1982, before I was old enough to enter grade school, my parents decided that they had outgrown H&R Block and created the company that has since become a household name in this country, Jackson Hewitt Tax Service. From day one, they were competing head to head against the company they had helped build, H&R Block. In 1997, just after I had graduated from high school, my father and I started Liberty Tax. My family was an integral part of developing all three of the major income tax brands. My aunts, uncles, cousins, and siblings, as well as my mom and dad, have all been in the industry helping to compete for first place over the years.

When my family started Jackson Hewitt Tax Service, we were competing with H&R Block, but we had no money. My parents put 25,000 dollars on a credit card to get Jackson Hewitt started. It wasn't an easy thing to do, but we had to in order to get it started. As the case is with most underdogs, we started in the hole – with no brand name and no one to count on but a few friends and ourselves. We were competing against a brand that had millions upon millions of dollars, an established brand name, and tens of thousands of loyal employees. It seemed as if there was no chance for us to compete on a level playing field with such a "top-dog."

In 1982, Jackson Hewitt debuted on the income tax preparation scene with six offices; H&R Block had nine thousand offices at that time. H&R Block had a huge marketing budget, tens of thousands of employees, and thousands of franchise owners that owned locations and invested their own time and money into growing their own businesses for H&R Block. They had an existing customer base that numbered in the millions for whom they were doing tax returns. They were the number one brand out there with no competition in sight, and we were definitely the underdog. How were we going to make it in this industry when it seemed as if all the odds were against us?

Chapter 2
Creating a Vision

Creating a vision is the first step of becoming an underdog competing in the world. You have to have a vision. It's very important. Henry Ford said it best: "You can achieve anything you want in life, but you can't achieve everything." To me that means that you have to focus on the thing you most want to achieve. As you focus on the thought of yourself achieving your *big* goal, it will inevitably result in identifying all of the little goals that you must achieve. It will also help you to see obstacles you must overcome and some of the opportunities to win or lose that you can bet life will to present you. If you're able to stay focused on the *big* goal, the prize, then the small decisions and actions that make all the difference in the world will become non-events. Then there's a good chance that you'll not only be able to hit a home run; you might knock it out of the park with a grand slam and win the battle against the bigger dogs that are out there.

Creating a vision creates a clear path for you to follow. You will know what you need to do every single day because that path will tell you what the next step is. It is a pathway to victory of what you're trying to accomplish. With a clear vision, you won't have to wake up in the morning and think: "Oh, I wonder what I'm going to do today. I wonder what's on the agenda today." The clear vision you have set will help you avoid things that take you away from your ambition.

While you're trying to get one thing accomplished, others will often bring their visions, brilliant ideas, great advice, and a multitude of other things that they want you to do that pertain to their visions. If you set your vision ahead of time, and you set it right, then you'll be able to follow that path and take life's distractions in stride. That will allow you to have what I call "laser focus" on what you want to achieve with your vision, your goals, and your dreams.

One question that I get asked all the time is how I pick my vision. What they really want to know is how they should pick their vision. …And that's the one question that I always answer with another question! Your vision needs to be something that you are passionate about, not something somebody else is passionate about. It needs to be something that you are driven towards, something that gives you that gut feeling that makes you want to strive for it. It needs to make you push but also push you. The more you believe in your vision, and the more that vision is related to what you're doing, the more likely it is that your vision will become your reality.

My mom always told me to go with my gut, and that's what I recommend when you're creating your vision. Think of something that is in your gut, something you believe in, and something that will drive you to become great. Perhaps most importantly, it needs to be something that makes you happy. Once you've made it in life, once you have all the money and fame that you always dreamed of, money becomes a secondary thing to what really makes you happy in life. In order to be effective at this, you need to go with the things that touch you in life, whether that's your children, your family or your spirituality with a greater being. You have to focus on the things that make you happy because, at the end of the day, we are doing what we do to create our own happiness. Therefore, you need to make sure that your vision pertains to something that you believe in wholeheartedly and drives you to be happy and to succeed in life. If you allow your vision to be shaped by those things, at the end of the day, it's going to make you the happiest person alive.

A great friend of our family and New York Times best-selling author of the book *Vision: Your Pathway to Victory*, Gordon D'Angelo, says that vision is important because:

> Everybody has ideas. Everybody has thousands of thoughts every day. That creates a lot of confusion and misdirection. A vision is a very specific target with a deadline. It is an end-result that's definable and measurable. When you have that, you can tell yourself at the end of the day and the end of the week, "I did succeed." It keeps you focused on getting to that end-result because the fog never goes away. The ten thousand thoughts that go through your mind each day are always there. The phone calls, the emails, the texts are there. But the vision is how you measure yourself.
>
> Once you start to write it down, you're saying, "I want the freedom to determine my own outcome, my own direction in life." If you're serious about your life and serious about the end-result, you have to have a vision. Write it down and share it. A vision

also attracts. It's a very tangible attraction or positive energy. When you have a vision, people understand what they're supposed to do. People will gravitate toward it.

When you look at football teams, baseball teams, and other professional teams, you see that they have a vision. They want to win the game, the Super Bowl, or the World Series. They're not saying, "Hey, lets text each other every day and let's go out in the field and play." No, they have a deal; "Let's win the game." Their goal is to win the game. What is our measurement, and what game are we trying to win? Or are we just trying to play? There is a big difference between the two. Vision separates the wannabes from the people who are going to win.

The end-result of your vision could be anything. However, it has to be definable, and it has to be transferrable. For example, if you say that you want to have a successful business, that's not definable. You have to define it in terms of, for example, "I want to make a hundred thousand dollar profit per year," or "I want to have so much gross revenue."

That's definable. If somebody says, "I want to have three employees," that's not definable either because what is the end-result of the employees? Each employee will produce a minimum of 40,000 dollars of gross revenue and 35,000 dollars of profit.

The more you define it, the more realistic it is, and the more likely it is to become true. I always associate this with a grocery list. Imagine that you send me to the store to get some food. I come back with a cantaloupe and some sweet pepper, but you say, "I didn't want that." I go back to the store and bring home a potato and a pork chop, but you didn't want a potato and a pork chop either. Nobody knows what you want. If you give me a list, however, and say, "I want three medium sized eggs, four pieces of toast, and one pound of watermelon," then I'll get it. Anybody can take that list and come back with the exact end-result. The very key to the definable intention is clear because it also makes it transferable. The transferability is important because why wouldn't you access another energy in the accomplishment of the end-result?

At Liberty Tax, our vision from day one has been to be the number one tax preparation company in the *universe* by 2020. It's a clear, concise and astronomically lofty vision! For nearly twenty years, we have steadily closed the gap and are on the path to achieving that lofty goal. From the onset, we painted a picture of what it looks like when we're there, and how many tax returns, how many offices, and how many people doing tax returns it will take to get there. In that way, we visualize ourselves at the end-result while considering and conquering all of the milestones, obstacles, and opportunities, which have and will continue to come up along our journey to the top.

What does it look like once you've done this? You have to paint a picture of how it's going to look. Who is the future "you" going to be when the journey is done? How will you feel about yourself once you've turned your vision into reality?

In the past, a lot of people have used a tool called vision boards to visualize their vision. The better you paint the picture of your vision and your dream, the more likely it is that you'll be able to achieve it. A vision board is a collage of pictures that you put together. The pictures illustrate all the different things for which you're looking. If I wanted to be the number one shortstop in the world, I'd have one picture of myself in the Hall of Fame, one of myself doing three thousand hits, and one of myself in my baseball uniform. The vision board will help you figure out what end-result you want.

As I mentioned before, our vision at Liberty Tax is to be number one in the universe by 2020. In fact, we call it "the 2020 Vision" because we can see our vision so clearly. By 2020, we're either going to make it or not. Many people and companies have a vision, a goal, or a dream without putting an end date on it. By not putting an end date, you won't be able to put pressure on yourself before it's too late to make things happen. You have to make it happen today in order to hit those end-results. Your vision should have a timeline of when it needs to be completed. Without that, there is no pressure, no urgency, no burning, deep desire to get into it and make it happen. While we set out to be number one since the beginning, we put a date on our 2020 vision seven or eight years ago, and it has had a deep impact on me and all of the people that will contribute to making that vision a reality.

Creating a timeline with dates and numbers for when things have to be done by is essential in achieving your vision. It is not a new concept. It is embraced by many professions, including one that is centered on making visions become reality – Project Management. Perhaps the greatest Project Manager and Strategy guru I've ever met, Chad Corman, PMP, once told me that,

"Any project, by definition, must have a start and end-date. Without those two things, you have a license to fail because you don't even know how to define a win!" He went on to say that dates, as anyone knows, will come and go whether you achieve anything you've set out to do or not. Consider the "Central Artery/Tunnel Project (CA/T)," known unofficially as "Boston's Big Dig." This ambitious project was undertaken to reroute the key highway that ran through the heart of the city into a 3.5-mile (5.6 km) tunnel. The official planning phase started in 1982 and was scheduled to be completed in 1998 at a cost of 2.8 billion dollars. When the project concluded on December 31, 2007, The Big Dig had become the most expensive highway project in the U.S. It was not only plagued by nearly a decade worth of scheduling overruns, but the vision that was delivered had cost overruns, leaks, and design flaws that resulted in charges of poor execution and use of substandard materials, criminal arrests, and at least one confirmed death. After adjusting for 25 years of inflation, the project ended up costing over 14.6 billion dollars (8.08 billion in 1982 dollars equals a cost overrun of about 190 percent). It doesn't end there; The Boston Globe estimates that the real cost of the project will end up totaling over 22 billion dollars, and it will not be paid off until 2038. As a result of the death, leaks, and other design flaws, the group that oversaw the project agreed to pay 407 million dollars in restitution, and several smaller companies agreed to pay a combined sum of approximately 51 million dollars. Care to take a guess at who bore the majority of the cost of these overruns?

Henry and Richard Bloch had a vision of helping Americans file their tax returns despite tax laws that oftentimes seem to be written in a way that allows the IRS to take a piece of every dollar you make. In 1955, The Bloch brothers decided that they would open up against the IRS right across the street from them. The IRS was doing free tax returns, and they had people waiting in lines around their building, with waiting time up to two to three hours at times. What they did was open up a small retail business right across the street. They offered their services for five dollars a tax return, and they began their current vision of helping Americans fight against the big IRS.

At that point in life, Henry and Richard Bloch were the underdogs. They were two brothers who just wanted to help small business owners and individuals like you and me compete against the IRS. Most people probably don't think of it as competing against the IRS, but if you've lived your entire life in the tax industry, then you absolutely do.

Surveys say that every American wants taxes to be lower for them individually. In that sense, all of us are the underdogs against the IRS. We're the ones who have to fight against it, who have to go and prove our deductions against it. It is the big dog, and we are the underdogs.

Henry and Richard Bloch wanted to help the underdog people out there. Creating their vision enabled them to make a pathway to becoming the largest brick and mortar tax company in the world. Today, H&R Block is a multimillion-dollar company. They're an S&P 500 and are known as one of the top companies in the world right now. It all started with their vision.

When you create a vision, you need to challenge yourself and break boundaries. Instead of having a vision of being a short stop, you should have a vision of being a shortstop on the Los Angeles Dodgers or the New York Yankees. You have to set your goals and aspirations high. If you don't do that, you'll never strive for anything.

The vision you create should challenge yourself and others. It should break boundaries in many different ways. We won't take it seriously if we don't make it a challenge for ourselves. Don't be afraid to put your goals and visions high. Most people won't believe that you can do it. Only you have to believe in it, nobody else has to.

No matter what your vision is, it needs to be yours. You're going to find that your family members, your friends, your coworkers, etc. tell you that it can't be done. They might go against you and say that this vision is too big and that there's no way you can do it.

When my mom and dad started Jackson Hewitt Tax Service in 1982, they had six offices, and they were going to compete against H&R Block, that had nine thousand offices. When my father, four others, and I started Liberty Tax Service all over again, we had no offices, and we were going to compete against H&R Block's ten thousand offices and the two thousand Jackson Hewitt offices that had our name on it. It was a little bit insane for us to do that, but because we put our vision so high, it was easy for us to be driven.

In Jeff Olson's book, *The Slight Edge*, he talks about doing the right thing every day. It's a New York Times best-selling book and one of my favorites. If you haven't read it yet, I recommend it. It's about setting the goal that you strive towards on a daily basis and about doing the right thing every single day. *The Slight Edge* is that slight edge difference that you have over your competition and everyone else.

When you set a clear vision and make a clear path, you'll know what you need to do tomorrow. That way, you conquer the things that you need to in order to make it happen. Having a goal and vision to focus your energy helps you do the right thing every moment and every day because you know have a job to do. You have a goal and vision to achieve, and your gut is going to burn with the desire to get there.

Each and every day or moment of your life, people will try to pull you into their vision. Some of the other visions will work with yours, others won't. Staying focused on your vision is going to allow you to see what you need to do each and every day. It's simple, either it fits in your vision or it doesn't.

If you don't create that clear vision ahead of time, and somebody comes to you and says, "I have a business opportunity," "I have something that's going to work for us," or "I need you to do this for us," then you don't know whether that's going to coincide with what you're working on or not. Once you've set your vision, then it's a clear, concise, accurate thing, and it will be easy for you to tell whether the other thing coming your way will work with your vision or not. You've got to make sure that it's your vision and that it's all about you being you.

Gordon: I also think you need to write down your ideas. It's okay that you may write things down that don't end up being on your visionary pathway. You also have to be specific. For example, you may say, "I want to have a house on the water." That sounds like a good vision, except how many square feet do you want? What kind of body of water do you want it on, and what else specifically can you tell me? The more specific you are, the better.

When you start to complete your list, which is like a wish list, you'll say, "Oh! This is what I want," or "This isn't what I want." You may need to add something here or take something off the list there. It's okay to scrub it, edit it, and fine-tune it or alter it because you're authoring something that you're going to spend your time, your life, your money, your effort and your transfer of energy to accomplish. It's important to be spot on with your vision because if you're off a little bit, you get the wrong results, which, unfortunately, is happening among a lot of people.

To illustrate this, imagine that you walk to the warehouse of God, and a man there says, "Hey! How can I help you?" And you say, "Oh, I'd like a car." Then he gives you a car, but you say, "No, I want a red car." He gives you a red car, and you say, "No, I want a red sports car." He gets you a red sports car, and you say, "No, I want a red sports car with leather." The clearer you are, the faster you'll get it. Everything is in that warehouse. In the warehouse of life, everything exists. Every possibility exists. However, until you're clear on what you want inside that warehouse, you won't get it. Instead, you'll get your foggy answer.

It is also important to share your vision with everyone. Your vision doesn't become a reality until it's written down. I'll expand it even further. Your vision needs to be shared and talked about with the people you have lunch with, with the wait staff, when you're on vacation, with your friends, with your family, and with your co-workers. Everyone needs to hear about your vision.

I was able to see Tony Robbins in Miami several years ago, and many of his speeches come from an old philosophy. He talks about something called "NLP," or neuro-linguistic programming. Essentially, what that means is that the words you say program your brain; the words that you put out program your brain.

For example, our vision at Liberty Tax is to be number one in the universe by 2020. By myself, my father, and our co-workers saying it, eventually it will spread around the country, and it becomes a reality. We begin to believe it ourselves, but also other people begin to share in that vision with us, and they will help us achieve it. People will ask you about your vision and will want to join in on it. People that you don't even know will want to get into your vision.

Gordon: Vision is like a seed. If we have fifty seeds in our pocket, and we want to grow X amount of vegetables or food with these seeds, the seeds by themselves won't help you. They can grow, but they can't do so in your pocket. You've got to plant them. Also, seeds don't grow everywhere. Sometimes you don't know where they are going to grow. Therefore, you've got to keep planting, and the more you plant, the more likely growth will occur. In addition, the more variety of planting places you have, the more likely it is that you're going to have a wider way of demographic growth. If you only plant in certain little area, then your growth is confined to only that area.

I used to run in the park in Virginia Beach, Virginia. When I would come home, this kid by the name of Matt, I called him Matt "Wildcat" Fry, would be outside of his apartment every single day. He would dance and dance to his music. Many people would point fingers and laugh at him while many others complimented him on his street dance moves. Eventually, I went up to him and asked him, "Hey man, how are you doing? How's life going?" Then I asked him what goals, dreams, and visions he had. Today, Matt is one of our best Statute of Liberty dancers in Harrisburg, Virginia, which is not even where I originally discovered him!

Chapter 3
An Underdog is Born

My father always told me when I was growing up, "Danny, you have to help everyone, no matter whether they help you or they don't." Now, as a young kid, with a fairly thick head I might add, I often wondered how he could say this while it seemed to me like he wasn't helping me out much! As I grew older and connected with my father by working for him and later with him, I realized that the career path he had chosen, preparing income tax returns, was less about numbers and more about helping people than it might seem. When you prepare a tax return, you don't only help an underdog put the money they have earned back into their pocket, but you also eliminate the stress of having to deal with the bear, the IRS.

What it comes down to is being able to help people to the best of your ability. One of my favorite quotes is by Zig Ziglar, who said, "You can have everything in life you want if you will just help enough other people get what they want." My dad took this to heart, and doing tax returns is a great way to help people. He has been able to help millions of individuals just like you and me throughout his career. His leadership has shined across this industry as to change the dynamics on how taxes are prepared today and in the future. Focus on helping others first, and only then will you get all that you want in life.

As we grew businesses, our success allowed us to help people through other means as well. There have always been charities that we have been able to contribute to in big ways: Stop Hunger Now, Relay for Life, Cell Phones for Soldiers, Run for Life. The list goes on and on.

It is now very apparent to me why one of my father's loves in life is helping and giving back to people. Selflessness quite literally saved his life. When he was a young child, about three years old, his mother went to the store to buy some food, and he was left inside the car. In her rush, my grandmother might have forgotten to pull the emergency break, or little John-John, as he was back called then, had unbuckled himself and released the emergency brake. Either way, as he was sitting there by himself, the car started rolling backwards down a hill. As the car began to roll, a man came out of nowhere and pulled the brake. The man locked eyes with my three-year-old father and said, "Just sit there, son." Then he walked away. To this day, my father has been unable to figure out who that man was or repay him, but that memory is seared into his memory for all time. If the man hadn't done what he did that day, we wouldn't be telling the story that we're telling now. Because of this man, my father was able to learn at an early age that many people will help you in life, and you may never get an opportunity to return the favor, so help everyone.

My grandfather and namesake, Daniel Hewitt, worked while attending night school at the University of Michigan. As if juggling school and work was not enough, he met a beautiful woman and became the proud father of five children by the time he earned his degree. Eventually, his efforts and long hours of work earned him not only his MBA, but also a position as the Chief Financial Officer at the company he had worked at for many years. He settled into his new role but always felt like there was something more out there for him in this world.

When my father was growing up in the fifties and sixties, shopping centers began popping up all over the United States. My grandfather used to talk about buying a truck that could sweep the parking lots clean. His entrepreneurial fire was boiling from deep inside him. After many years, that entrepreneurial spirit won, and he left his job and decided to start his own business. His choice to take this risk would have a profound effect on the Hewitt family for generations to come. It is because of my grandfather's deep desire not to work for "the man" and instead start something, build something, create something that my father, aunts, and uncles all chose the paths they chose. He was an amazing man. Although he has passed away, his spirit will live inside us for years to come. He showed us how to Hewitt!

Chapter 4
The Top Dog

My dad was born in Highland Park, Michigan. When he was four, his family moved to Greece, a suburb of Rochester in New York. When he was fourteen, they moved on to Hamburg, a suburb of Buffalo. My mom was born in Elmira, New York, and she was raised there.

In the fall of 1968, my grandfather looked into opening an H&R Block in Upstate New York. Even then, it was known as "*the*" income tax franchise all across the United States. He was in the finance industry already, and he had always wanted to start his own business, so he was very excited about having the opportunity to do this.

A year later, in 1969, he finally had enough income to acquire an H&R Block franchise. However, when he called the company, they said, "We're going to put a company office there. Why don't you have your son take our course, and maybe he could work for us?" More than slightly disheartened about not being able to pursue his dream of the family owning their own business, my dad took the twelve-week H&R Block course. He learned how to do taxes and became a tax preparer. This brought two of my dad's favorite loves together.

My dad's first love, which I have already mentioned, is helping people. The second love of my dad's life is numbers. My grandfather was a CFO and accountant, and he was great with numbers. As my dad grew up, my grandfather always had a challenge, puzzle, or problem for him. You should see my dad now; he still loves numbers and is an absolute whiz at math. He instilled the love of numbers into me as well, and my childhood was so filled with challenges, puzzles, and problems that I eventually started challenging myself without giving it a second thought! I would have to multiply license plates as we drove by them. For example, if the license plate said ZGL-4357, I would have to times the four times the three, times the five, times the seven and give him the total of 420. Not only do I do this; my father did this; my grandfather did this, and now even my children love math. This simple "license plate game" has enabled my children, me, and many of our other family members to become labelled as gifted in math. Nine times out of ten I can beat people even when they use a calculator at simple math like multiplication, division, adding, and subtracting.

While my father has an incredible fondness for debating pretty much any topic, he loves arguing the law. Even today, after over 46 years in the tax business, he still discusses and argues income tax law to benefit the customers. Back in the day, not only did they not have computers, they did not have calculators either. They had to use old-fashioned adding machines. He could add, subtract, and multiply faster than virtually anyone, and he usually would get more praise for how fast he did his math than how much money he saved people.

From all this, I'm sure you can gather that my dad fell in love with the H&R Block and the income tax business in general. He started off working there part time while studying business at the University of Buffalo. In 1971, in his second season at H&R Block, his manager had an anxiety attack, and they asked my dad if he would leave college and run those locations while his manager was in the hospital.

One would think that the reason the manager had these panic attacks was because he was so far behind. He had over a thousand unprocessed returns. The tax preparer had finished the tax returns, but nobody had bothered to check the returns and prepare them to be mailed to the IRS and the appropriate states. My dad went in, hired staff, and cleaned it up. With the team that he built, he worked through every one of the backlogged returns to ensure that everyone's return was submitted on time. However, at the end of the season, when it was time for his manager to recommend him for a district manager or not, the manager said that my dad didn't get along with people, so he got laid off.

Have you ever felt like you just can't catch a break? Life keeps putting obstacles in your way to stop you from performing the way you want. It happens to all of us. You are not alone.

The period of unemployment was short-lived, however, and George Gunderson hired my dad back as an assistant manager. Later on, they changed Regional Directors to Bill Burtsmire. He hired both Gordon D'Angelo and my dad within the same month. He quickly saw that my dad had potential. In '75, he promoted him to the position of district manager of H&R Block in Ithaca, Elmira, and Corning. This district contained about twenty locations in total. Some were franchisee owned locations, and others were corporate owned. For the next four or five years, he was the district manager there, and his goal was to become

Regional Director. He wasn't thinking of competing with H&R Block yet. He lived, breathed, and drank the Kool Aid of H&R Block.

During my dad's early years at H&R Block, he met my mother. She started out as a tax preparer as well. In 1972, she took an H&R Block test class, but she was pregnant with her third child at the time, so she had no intention of working. However, she had made some friends with the people in her class at H&R Block, and the next year, the teacher called her and asked if she would help teach a class. Though she had never worked in an office and had only been a student, when this opportunity came along, she said, "Sure, why not." The advantage was that she didn't have to pay for the class, though she didn't get paid for teaching. After that, she started working as a part-time tax preparer and enjoyed it so much that she stuck with it for the next forty years! Still to this day, my mom is asked to come in as an expert and assist owners on how to create more efficient processes in their tax offices. She is a tax legend all on her own.

After her third child was born, my father was invited to become part of a newly developed Regional Director training program. Out of the five hundred district managers in the company, they wanted 25 who they would bring in every three months into the headquarters in Kansas City to train. That way, when they needed to replace one of the Regional Directors, there would be a core group that could take their place with very little ramp up time. However, my dad was dedicated to his family. After talking it over with my mother, he determined that moving away from Elmira was not in the best interest of his family, so he turned down the offer. Even though that was his dream at the time, he couldn't take that opportunity if it meant that his family would suffer. My father has always taught me that your family has to come before your business. Sometimes it was easier said than done. But at the end of the day, we do what we do in life to help our loved ones have a better life. He had no idea how much he was going to do this back then.

About a year and a half later, he got a call from the divisional director who managed a third of the company, Harry Buckley, who said, "Would you be interested in interviewing for an intern position for the Philadelphia Regional Director?" That was close enough to Elmira, only a four-hour drive, so they could move there and still be close to the family. He went down for the interview and was offered the Regional Director position on the spot. This time he couldn't turn it down. This time he was ready to say yes.

My dad became the youngest Regional Director up to that time. He managed 250 locations with over two thousand employees reporting to him. Over the twelve or thirteen years that my parents, my grandfather, my aunt, and my uncles worked there, we all learned how H&R Block operated. We were involved as much as possible. It was our life, our dream, and our mission to help others.

When my dad started working at H&R Block, they had grown from their one location in Kansas City to about three thousand locations all around the United States. Then, by the time he left, they had about nine thousand locations. In other words, my family was able to see the growth from three thousand to nine thousand. They owned, operated, worked, developed, trained, and did everything they could with H&R Block. My family was in the right place at the right time to see the "Top Dog" being formed.

H&R Block was the top dog in town. They had more offices than any other company in the industry by ten times. No competitors had even two hundred offices to compete against them. They had a virtual monopoly in the industry. There was H&R Block, the IRS, and what you would call "mom and pops." Henry and Richard created a way for Americans to get their taxes done by people who had a desire to help. The whole company was on top of the world.

From 1955 to 1980, in just 25 years, H&R Block grew the company from one location to nine thousand locations spread around in all fifty states of the U.S. They became a powerhouse bigger than anyone else. Early on, in 1955, they were the underdog. Then they became the leader. They thought that nobody could beat them. They created their dream and their vision, and they became the Top Dog in the Tax Industry.

Have you ever thought that you were on top of your game? Have you ever thought that you couldn't get knocked down? You begin to feel confident, and it is a great feeling when it happens. When you're a leader, people look up to you. People are gunning for you, but at the same time, they are trying to be like you when they grow up.

We've all heard the old saying, "the only guarantees in life are death and taxes." In reality, there is one more guarantee in life – change. Change is inevitable and constant in all of our lives. No matter what happens this moment, the next moment will be different. That third guarantee dictates that no one can be number one forever. Life is about the yin and the yang, the highs and the lows, giving and taking. Some moments are great and some not so great, to say the least. The Top Dog today will obviously be beat one day down the road. It may not be tomorrow. It may not be next week or next month, but it will happen. It always does. First place doesn't last forever for anyone. Eventually, someone will come and take it from you, so be on your toes and always continue to improve. When we stop improving, we start sliding backwards and make it easier for our competitors to catch us.

Chapter 5
Being an Underdog Takes Work!

When I was growing up, a lot of people called me "squirrel." As a squirrel, it's extremely important to be on top of your game. The squirrels gather food and put it away for the winter time when the weather becomes bad and food is scarce. They make sure that they have enough to eat for themselves and their families when times are getting tough. You need to save up in the times when things are going very well. That way, when it gets tough, you can lean on what you've squirreled away.

We all want to be the top dog. We all want that moment to shine. When you're not number one, all you can think about is trying to be number one. You deeply desire the feeling of crossing the finish line before everyone else. We strive for that moment for when we can be number one.

When you're number two, you're the first person who lost to number one. You're the first person behind them. When you're number three, you're the second person behind them. When you're number one, everybody below is looking up at you. The person who is number ten isn't looking at number five, number three, or number two, he's looking at number one.

My son, who is now eighteen years old, was able to learn a valuable lesson in his middle school years. You see, he always wanted to beat me in a foot race. We would race everywhere we went when he was growing up. When he started on the track team at school, he was quickly one of the fastest kids on the team. There was one other kid there who was called "the all-star." We all know the type. He ran like the wind. He won city, state, and eventually went on to nationals. He was better than everyone else. He was the best. I advised my son to "race that guy as often as you can if you want to win." As usual, our children don't listen to us. Do you blame them? People don't listen to their parents, friends, family, and even God. Why would I assume he would listen now? He showed up to practice each and every day shying away from "the all-star" and only racing the other kids he could beat already. Eventually, he quit track without ever challenging the boy.

When he was fifteen years old, he finally beat me across the finish line. That happened during a 5k race, 3.1 miles, which was to raise money for autism. At around two miles, my son looked at me and said, "Dad, I'm taking off." He beat me by about four minutes. At the end of the race, I was exhausted, but all I knew at that time was that my boy had finally done it. He had been the underdog for many years, but now he had become the winner. It was a great feeling to watch my son become the top dog and finally learn the lesson of never giving up and always keep getting back up. Even though he didn't keep racing against "the all-star," he was determined to beat his dad finally. Son, I love you for this and so much more.

We all want to win the race. We all want to grow up to become number one. How big is the difference between the gold medalist and the silver medalist? It's usually a millisecond difference. There's not a huge gap between number one and number two. They both work extremely hard to become Top Dogs. They strive for what they want. They do their best, but all they want to be is number one. It is such a close call that sometimes it's even hard to tell who actually won the race.

When the gap between two parties is miles and miles apart, then the underdog is created. The underdog is the competitor thought to have little or no chance to win at a contest or fight. It depends on there being a big difference between the two, like you finished tenth, and they finished first.

Have you ever felt like an underdog? If so, how did it make you feel? How did it make you feel when it looked like all the odds were against you, and no one was going to be able to help you achieve what you wanted to? The opponent may have seemed too fast, too strong, too soft or too big. You believed that everything was against you. Then what you have to do is fight harder and practice more.

Do you shy away and accept defeat, or do you go for first place? In order to succeed, you have to work harder. You have to work longer hours. You have to practice more. If you're on the high school sports team and another guy was chosen to start, what would you do to become a starter?

No matter what obstacles get into your path along this journey to become number one, stay your course. Stay focused on being number one. Stay on that vision. Paint the picture of what it looks like to be number one. The better you can visualize your end-result, the more likely it is to happen. Everyone has speed bumps in life and obstacles to overcome. We all have things that come by us and knock us down. Squirrel when times are good and hustle twice as hard when things are down.

During my parents' careers at the H&R Block, they saw the company grow vastly. H&R Block, originally the "underdog," began to become a big hit during the seventies. They became the "Top Dog" which monopolized the tax industry and dominated every city that they went to.

By growing up around tax preparers, I saw a lot of what their working life entailed. They are seasonal employees. They don't make millions and millions of dollars for working four months in a year. They don't get sick pay. They don't get holiday pay. They don't get time off. They don't get paid in the off-season. They are just seasonal employees, regular people like you and I. They don't get life insurance, health insurance, or any benefits like full-time employees do. They don't get 401K plans or retirement plans. Most tax preparers are average Joes, normal people – no different than you and I. My mom, Linda Hewitt, will share a few words about how it used to be:

> *Linda*: Years ago, we had a very small pay, and then we got paid commissions, so we wanted to do as many tax returns as fast as we could. We had to ask each

person several questions to determine what was the right thing for them to do. When it was busy, we wrote all the figures in as fast as we could, and at the end of the day, we would finish everything up. We could stay four or five hours after our shift was done to finish up our work. Because we got paid commissions, which was the way we had to work in order to make any money.

Successful tax preparers don't make tons of money, and they don't do it for the money. I did it for most of my life, and I got paid sometimes, other times I didn't. But I would have done the same job for free because the person that makes a good tax preparer is a person who cares about people and wants every person to get back as much money, or pay the least amount of taxes that would be legally possible. For the most part, tax preparers are people who are not in a position to have money. They are someone who truly cares about others and want to do what is best for them. Most of the tax preparers I have met, and I have met many, are some of the most helpful people you will ever meet.

Also, completing tax returns in the seventies was a lot different than it is today. Every tax return was done by hand. Every preparer had multiple pencils and erasers. As I mentioned, they didn't even have calculators. They used to have manual adding machines with paper tape, and they had to do a paper tape calculation called Zero Check tape on every tax return.

Computers in the seventies were in many cases as big as rooms. Families did not have computers at home. In addition, there was no such thing as cellphones, GPS, email, or internet back then. If you wanted to find out where to do business in the seventies, you would look it up in the phonebook. Sometimes you would ask a friend or family member to get their recommendation on the best business to go to. If you needed an oil change, or you wanted to go to the best restaurant in town, or you wanted to get your taxes done, you didn't have as many options as we do today. Back then, there was only one phonebook. It was called, "The Yellow Book." You can probably still remember their tagline: "Let your fingers do the walking."

In many ways, life was different back then. In the early eighties, the first PC's began to come out. They were now being sold first to businesses and then marketed to normal people and families. When sales to individuals started to catch on, people in the computer industry started promoting the idea that personal computers were going to be at homes in the future, but the public at large was skeptical, to say the least.

It was at the time when my dad was working as a Regional Director at H&R Block that my grandfather came to him and said, "Let's computerize taxes." My dad answered, "Dad, the computer can't even beat me in chess, how am I going to put the tax system on the computer?" My mom was skeptical as well. She said, "You can't ask enough questions."

My grandfather was still determined to do it, so he left his job as CFO of a public company, bought two H&R Block franchises, and then he began programming. He saw these new machines as an opportunity to enhance the performance and speed of completing tax returns. He saw a huge opportunity to get the tax returns done faster, get the customers' money back more quickly, and cut down the time they would have to wait while they were doing their tax returns. He had a vision of something that could improve and change the world of tax preparation as we knew it.

About six months later, my dad left H&R Block, and they founded Hew Tax. My dad had always felt like he could do just about anything he set his mind to. From the time he was about twelve years old until he was twenty, he had had a very rocky relationship with his dad (as many young men do), so the opportunity to work with him and get their relationship back on track was exciting to him. They got the company that my grandfather had worked in before he started on his own to invest a few hundred thousand dollars to get this new company off the ground and running.

My whole family went to work writing the computer code. Shortly after, they launched the first tax software ever. My dad was in his thirties back then. Many of us in our thirties, if we have a dream and vision, can be a bit naïve. We think about getting rich quickly. The older we get, we realize that it doesn't happen that way. It takes time, patience, and perseverance, and we see that there are a lot of things to overcome in order to achieve our goals and dreams.

My father, young as he was, took his tax software back to H&R Block to sell it for the big payoff. He thought that this was his chance, his opportunity to get rich quickly. He was not making a lot of money at the time, but he thought that he could quickly make millions of dollars on the software. It seemed like a no-brainer. He was going to walk right in there and within seconds have everything.

However, that would not be the case. H&R Block asked for a bid, but by this time, some "Top Dogs," Texas Instruments and IBM, had caught wind of the innovative way to prepare taxes and were already testing for H&R Block for free. Therefore, H&R Block asked my dad, "Well, can you test for free?" My dad replied, "No. They're going to get an equipment contract worth tens of millions of dollars if they convince you to use their software in their office, and we're just a software company, not a hardware company." He gave them a bid, and they said, "Well, you have a unique way of treating this, and your software is different and interesting, but we don't want to pay anything." Knocked down as my dad was, he went back to the drawing board once again.

Remember, by this time H&R Block had the nine thousand locations. They were the Top Dog and had a monopoly of the industry. There was nobody bigger. In the world of tax business, they were the biggest company. At that time, there was no such thing as doing taxes on the internet. There was no Turbo Tax or any other competition. They were the one everybody knew.

We had to prove that the tax industry would be computerized. It was up to us to show that there was a better way to file your taxes than mailing them in and waiting six to eight weeks to get your refunds. My mom and dad, like many entrepreneurs, thought and believed that they could be better than their current boss. That was their vision, and that was what they set out to do.

H&R Block ended up testing the other software and failing. In their annual report a couple of years later, they wrote: "People asked us why we don't computerize? We say, 'Why should we?' We tested it, but the customer doesn't care, and it doesn't save us any money, so we're never going to computerize." Was this our chance?

When H&R Block turned down our software, we started asking ourselves what we were to do. Our plans and our dream were crushed. Was our plan even going to work? Were we even doing the right thing? Everyone was telling us, "No, you can't do it. It's not going to work."

Have you ever thought of things regarding your job that would help enhance performance and profitability? Have you ever taken it to your executives, your bosses, and said, "Hey! I have an answer that will take us to the next level." If so, did your executives listen to you? Did they take your idea and run with it, or did they just push you off? Many people become entrepreneurs for the simple fact that they believe they can do it better than their boss and their higher up's. They possess a certain "I can do it better" mentality.

In our case, we had the software and knowledge, but we had no money. Should we just throw in the towel and let it go? Should we just give up since other people didn't believe in our dreams? Could we take the step? Could we take the leap of faith? With no money and no office, only a little software, were we going to try to compete against this big company that was worth several hundred million dollars and had tens of thousands of employees and millions of customers? They were the brand name that everyone knew. They had a household name. How could my family, who were just average Joes, compete with this big name-brand company? We had to make a decision. We had to decide whether we would compete or just throw away our dreams and give up.

This is Gordon D'Angelo's advice on how to overcome obstacles and stay focused on your vision even when everyone else tells you that you can't do it:

There's a great verse in the Bible that says, "When tribulation occurs, God will be the cause." It does not say, "If tribulation occurs," it says, "when." You are going to have tribulations in life and many of them. Each of us will have trials and tribulations to overcome, it is inevitable. However, my favorite four-letter word is *next*. You have to ask yourself, "What do I have to do next? When life throws obstacles at you, you need to ask yourself: What do I do *next*? Winners get back up when they get knocked down. They get back up to figure out what they need to do *next* to accomplish what they set out to accomplish."

If you are driving home, you know your destination. Your end-result is 25 Prospect Street. You know where you live; you know your address, but the road's blocked. What do you do? You begin by going around the corner. Then you discover that that's blocked too. You go around another corner, and then you see that that's blocked as well. Finally, you find a way home, but it's flooded. Then you'll say to yourself, "It's flooded, but I have to go to 25 Prospect Street." As long as you know where you're going, you will keep trying to get there, and you will find a way. It's only when you don't know where you're going that you don't know what to do next.

Chapter 6
Underdogs *Must* Seize Opportunity

When you are an underdog, you have to give it everything you've got. Sometimes it will feel like everyone is against you – that nobody is in your corner. You're fighting Mike Tyson. I get it. I understand. He's bigger, stronger and faster. Your opponent may have more money, more locations, and better brand name than you. I know how it feels; it is as if you have no chance to win. And yet all you can taste, all you can think about, all you can do when you sleep, drink, eat, rest, work, play, practice, and prepare is fight to be number one. Underdogs are fighters. Underdogs have a little umpf in them. Underdogs feel it in their bodies, their heart, their stomach, and in every fiber of their being. If you're an underdog, you have a chance

So many people in life don't know when they are the underdog. They don't know what it takes to be an underdog. Therefore, we will go over what the initial thought process is when you realize, "Oh, wow, I am the underdog. The top dog is so much bigger, stronger and faster than me. How in the world am I ever going to compete?"

My parents and grandparents decided that they wanted to compete against H&R Block. Before anyone else in the industry, we had the technology to complete tax returns on the computer. This allowed us to do the job faster than anyone else. The computer was becoming more and more affordable for businesses and people in general. Apple, Tandy, and all the different computer companies made the computers smaller, and they were striving to create the computers as we know them today.

However, my parents did not have a lot of money to start a big project. We were just middle class Americans. My mom grew up in a small house in a blue collar town, and her father worked as a truck driver. Before she was a senior in high school, they moved to a farm, but her dad continued driving trucks in addition to taking care of the animals on the farm. My father's family didn't have a lot of money either. When my dad was in middle school, he only had two pairs of jeans. He would wear one pair one day, and then his mom would wash them, and he would wear the other pair the next day. Until he was fourteen, the family of seven lived in a three bedroom ranch with one bathroom.

Though my family had the desire to start their own business, they had no money. As I said before, my mom was a tax preparer most of her adult life. She didn't make a lot of money. She came from a family of average or even less than average income. My father had clawed his way up the corporate ladder to become a Regional Director and had more of a permanent position with H&R Block, but he also came from a one income family with four siblings.

In the Wall Street Journal, six tax offices were listed for sale in Norfolk, Virginia, operating under the name Mel Jackson Tax Service. They had been owned by a married couple, but Mel, the husband had died a few years before, and the wife wasn't involved in the company. She wanted to sell it, take her proceeds out, and live her life without worrying about those six tax offices.

All we needed to make this deal happen was a few hundred thousand dollars. Any top dog would easily be able to do that. But if we made this deal happen, we would instantly become the underdog against a very big company.

Now, how could we make it happen? We had the software and computers, but H&R Block had the locations, clients, and preparers. They had an existing business. We had a desire to compete, but we didn't have the funds to do it. We were stuck on how we were going to raise the money in order to begin competing.

In search for a solution, my dad went to his best friend, Gordon D'Angelo. They had both gone to the University of Buffalo, and once they met there, it was an instant "bromance." In other words, they hit it off very well and became lifelong friends. Gordon and his family had grown up in the poor part of the town themselves, so Gordon knew what is was like to not have an abundance of money.

Back in the day, when they did taxes by hand, my father had been able to get Gordon a job at H&R Block. And so it happened that Gordon became a tax preparer at age eighteen. Three years later, they were interviewing a series of people for a position as a District manager in a part of Western New York. He applied, and they liked him. They said, "Well, we're interviewing nine other people as well. All of them are older and have more experience, etc." Then Gordon said, "But I have a lot of confidence and optimism, and my ability to learn and get projects done is unmatched." They were thankful for that and said, "We'll let you know next week." Then Gordon said, "Well, you're probably going to call me tomorrow." "Why?" they replied.

"To start," he said. The next day they did indeed call him to start.

Gordon: I was 21 years old then, and at that point in time, I was the youngest District manager in the United States for H&R Block. In my first season, my confidence was great, but my results were horrible. I couldn't be happy because I live by results. So I worked a lot harder the following years. I became much more focused on marketing and getting the entire team involved in the success rather than just me. We established some fantastic growth numbers in an area in Buffalo, New York, despite an unemployment rate there of nearly twenty percent at that time. Consequently, I was promoted to another city. Between the two cities, I had record growth and profit ratios for running corporate stores.

Gordon became quite important at H&R Block, but he didn't want to go too far with them. He is a visionary person, and he started doing financial planning back in the seventies while doing tax returns. He quickly realized that he had a gift of helping people with their finances and helping them achieve great success as far as financial concerns went.

In order to buy Mel Jackson Tax Sevice, Gordon and my dad put together what we today call the "twelve disciples" – investors in what is now known as Jackson Hewitt Tax Service. These twelve investors put all the money up for the company to get started. My father only owned five percent of it. The other investors were people who had trusted my family and Gordon in the past. Seeing how they had worked before, they wanted to bet on this underdog. They were willing to risk five, ten, even twenty thousand dollars each to bet on the underdog because that's who they wanted to compete with. With the help of the investors, we were able to buy Mel Jackson Tax Service.

Although it was a great feat for us to have been able to buy this company, it was not a very modern establishment at the time:

Linda: It was probably one of the most archaic things you've ever seen in your life when we bought it. We came with our Apple computers under our arms and said that everybody is going to use them. The people working there had been doing tax returns with carbon paper, ink pens, and small bottles of bleach. If they made mistakes, they used the bleach to correct them.

It wasn't anywhere near as sophisticated as H&R Block had been, but they got by.

Right off the bat, we took the six stores and expanded to seven. We put computers and our software in every store. Compared to our competitors, we could complete tax returns in lightening speed. We were blowing people out of the water. The others were still using the old techniques of doing the tax returns by hand, erasing numbers, and typing them on calculators while we were using the top-of-the-line, best computers in the system. There was no such thing as electronic filing back then. We could only compete in tax returns by completing the tax returns faster than they could. That was our difference.

This is how my dad, John Hewitt, describes how we benefitted from being the first tax service using computers:

Using computers gave us quite an advantage. The computer was a decision tree software base that would do a thorough interview to make sure that nothing was missed on the tax return. That made the inexperienced preparer look like the most experienced preparer, and it helped set a structure and a platform that ensured that every customer got a thorough interview.

We instantly saw that we were dominating over the competition, even with just eleven stores and markets because people didn't have to wait in long lines. They didn't have to wait for the preparer to ask all these questions. It was done very quickly because of the computers we had.

We continued to grow the company regionally with forty plus locations. We were still named Mel Jackson Tax Service, but we changed the name to Jackson Hewitt once we were expanding outside what we call "the Hampton Roads" area. The Hampton Roads is the seven cities surrounding Norfolk, Virginia, including Virginia Beach, Chesapeake, Hampton, Newport News, and Portsmouth. Once we went outside that area, we decided to change the name to Jackson Hewitt.

Trying to compete with H&R Block took a lot of hard work. We lived in our offices. We did whatever it took to compete. Every time we had family functions, we were talking about Jackson Hewitt. We were doing whatever it took to compete. Even at the dinner table, we had to listen to Jackson Hewitt commercials. I remember "Let Jackson Hewitt help you do it if you want your refund in a hurry.

We would listen to every radio and TV commercial that was running.

I remember one of the most annoying TV commercials that we ever did. We called it "Me Too." It was a thirty-second or sixty-second commercial where we tried to get the word "me too" in it as many times as possible. For example, someone would say, "I went to Jackson Hewitt and got my taxes done," and then this lady would answer, "Me too!" Then the next person would say, "I got a big refund at Jackson Hewitt." Then it would be, "Me too!" over and over again.

My father is one of those guys who gets to work before every employee and is there after every employee. Many times on Thanksgiving, Christmas day, or New Year's Eve, or any holiday that's going on, you'll find my father at work. He has a crazy drive to win, and if you get to know him, you'll see it.

He would go to breakfasts, lunches, and dinners. For almost every day of my life, he's been in a business meeting of some sort through his break – breaks that people normally take away from work. My dad has always chosen to work non-stop.

Just as we had learned at H&R Block, we started franchising our business. In order to grow their company to nine thousand plus locations, H&R Block had franchised their locations, and that's how they grew. So we said, "You know what? We're going to do exactly what they did in order to achieve the results that they achieved."

Remember, we risked everything to get into this deal. My mother and father left their paychecks to compete against the top dog. They put in 25,000 dollars on a credit card, and we uprooted our family from New York to Virginia to make it happen. The fruit of our labor was that once the IRS opened the electronic file window, we had been in the software development side for longer than anyone in the industry.

Linda: When the IRS first started electronic filing in 1986, we were the source that the IRS came to. They came to our offices. We wrote a test for other companies to pass. In other words, we were hugely instrumental in electronic filing becoming a part of everyday life.

What a victory for the underdog

Chapter 7
Underdogs Grow or Die

We grew for several reasons: because we were a young, hungry underdog; because we knew we could do it better than the top dog; because knew we had a chance; and because we knew we had reasons and ideas that were going to beat them. Our technology was superior to anyone's in the early days because we had done it for a longer time than anyone else. We had a dream and vision, and people grabbed hold of it and went along side of us. They saw themselves betting their paychecks, their lives, and everything they had on the underdog.

John: In 1988, we acquired a deal with Montgomery Ward. We had fifty offices in three states, and Montgomery Ward had two hundred. The company that previously had been at Montgomery Ward was the second largest tax preparer; they had about fifty storefronts, and in addition, they were in the two hundred Montgomery Ward locations in thirty states.

When they sold us that contract, we didn't acquire their store fronts, but we did acquire the contract for Montgomery Ward. That propelled us into thirty states and three hundred locations. We went from a huge leap from fifty to three hundred locations, and that gave us a national base of millions of people coming through the Montgomery Ward store and giving us brand new recognition.

Linda: All of the sudden we went from a little regional company to a nationwide company, and in many ways it was the catalyst that pushed us to the next level. It also was a terrifying time because we were not able to manage those offices. There were too many, and some were too small, so in the middle of the tax season, we had to close down small offices because financially it did not make sense to leave them all open.

John: Then in '93, we visited Wal-Mart for the first time, and it took me until '95 to get in there. H&R Block was testing at about a hundred Wal-Marts, and they said, "We don't even know if we like the tax business yet. If we do though, we always like to have two vendors." I left that meeting feeling pretty good. If H&R Block did a good enough job, Wal-Mart would want a tax service, and there was only one other company to pick: Jackson Hewitt, because we already had over eight hundred locations, and no one else had a hundred. I was, however, afraid that H&R Block might ruin the opportunity for us.

Fortunately, we were able to get in for the first time in '95. By '97, we got H&R Block thrown out of Wal-Mart, and Jackson Hewitt was the only company in Wal-Mart for about five years from 1998.

We were gaining market shares against H&R Block. They were still un-computerized, and electronic filing, which began in 1996, dragged the H&R Block back into the computer. We, however, were ahead of the game; we were already computerized. We were so much more advanced than them. Electronic filing propelled us at an incredible pace in the late eighties and early nineties and gave us a competitive advantage over H&R Block. We were feeling very, very good about our prospects.

We were now opening offices in cities all around the U.S. and truly competing against the top dog. The Montgomery Ward deal alone tripled our office count with Jackson Hewitt. We sold over eight hundred franchises to owners who invested their retirement, their 401K plans, their loans on their houses, and their family's money. They competed alongside us and became an underdog themselves. When they became franchise owners, not only did they invest in the big company, the Jackson Hewitt Corporation, as an underdog, they invested in themselves as an underdog, and we were betting on them at the same time. Little did we know this was one of the biggest secrets to our success over the years: betting on underdogs.

Things were going well for us. In 1994, our original investors along with other new investors and my father took the company public; that and having the shares traded on the public stock exchange seemed like what we were supposed to do. We had over a one thousand offices at that time. In other words, we had grown from six to one thousand offices. Many people would think that we were the top dog, but in this industry, we were still just an underdog against a company that had nine times the amount of locations and hundreds of times more money than us.

When we took the company public, we sold shares for ten dollars and did well for a good time. The price started going up. It looked good for the first couple of years. Then we hit a bump in the road. We had a tough tax season. It was in the middle of the nineties. H&R Block had caught up with us in technology, and they now started to compete against us. We were finally a threat to the top dog. Now they were paying attention to us. They put in efforts against us to make sure that we weren't stealing leases, taking office spaces, and competing over the same employees. We were truly becoming a contender.

However, in 1995, changes in the IRS created an uproar in our industry.

Linda: The IRS decided that they were not going to give a debt indicator anymore. When the loan system first came out, they would give a letter attached to each tax return. That letter would give you an idea of whether or not you owed back IRS payments, whether you owed back child support or what's called FMS, which is the Federal Management System. That could be payment loans, or it could be any federal or state agency that you owe money to. They would give us an indicator of that so that we knew when people were not going to get back their money, or at least all of their money. It gave the banks a heads up as to who they could lend money to and who they couldn't.

Because they stopped doing that, the banks got a much larger risk at stake because they no longer knew who was going to get their money and who wasn't. It put a hamper on the super-fast refunds, refund interest paying loans. That is what hurt more than anything.

That hurt all the tax businesses because the tax industry had developed from people's need to know taxes into a loan business where they chose whoever could get you the fastest refund. If there was any loyalty, that's where their loyalty was. They didn't care about the quality of their returns anymore. They cared about how fast they could get their refund, and the IRS took that away.

We were opening hundreds of offices at a time, and as many entrepreneurs find when they are in this situation, we grew too big too fast. While we had grown so fast overnight, our stock plummeted down over fifty percent in a very short time. All the investors got nervous.

What happens in a publicly traded company when stocks go down is that the stockholders want to make a change. They want their stocks to go back up. Then they look at the CEOs, and the executives are the first people they want to replace. They begin to vote, and the shareholders say, "Bring in new management. Let's bring in some new blood into this situation and make it happen." The new management's job as acting CEO in a publicly traded company is to do three things: Raise the revenue, lower the expenses, and increase stockholder equity.

The new management decided that they were going to position the company to sell to a bigger, publicly traded company. Once they announced this, the stock rose very quickly again. It pushed my father out as acting CEO. The old CEO had driven the stock down by fifty percent. Therefore, they replaced him with a new CEO. It seemed like it was the right thing to do. Since the stock rose quickly, it had to be the correct answer, right?

My father was still chairman of the board at Jackson Hewitt, but the new CEO didn't sit right with him. He had concerns, and as you can imagine, my father was still very emotionally attached to his baby, Jackson Hewitt.

John: The new CEO was a man who lacked integrity. In my mind, honesty and integrity is telling the truth about something that has happened in the past. Integrity is about being committed. If you say that you're going to do something, it's your word. It's the old handshake deal. The guy who needs 75 pages of legalese to honor the deal, and perhaps don't honor it even then, lacks integrity.

Because of the lack of integrity in the new CEO, I resigned. Afterwards, people would come up to me and ask, "Why aren't you depressed? Why aren't you upset?" I would answer, "You need to understand that when I'm on the court and playing the game, I'm one hundred percent engaged. In this business, I'm one hundred percent engaged. But if God came to me and said, "Well, I'll tell you what. I'll take your business, or I'll take your son?" I'd I say, "Well, take the business." I mean, it's only a business. It's God first, then family, and then business.

We had started Jackson Hewitt to become number one. What just happened? Cendant Corporation came in and purchased Jackson Hewitt in 1997 for 483 million dollars. It only cost us a few hundred thousand dollars in 1982 when we started it, so it was a huge gain for everybody. Many investors made gains as high as four hundred times their original investments. Five thousand dollars invested in the company in 1982 was worth two million dollars when the company sold to Cendant Corporation. Wouldn't you want your money too?

Cendant Corporation owned several franchisor groups, and they believed that they could consolidate the business practices and quickly lower expenses as well as grow Jackson Hewitt. They could consolidate the accounting practices and the legal practices, and they thought that if they were using their hotel chain for any legal work, they could do the same with the Jackson Hewitt stock. It seemed like a great move for them.

Have you ever thought, "This is the one that's going to knock me down and make me retire my hat in this field? This is a bump in the road that I'm just not going to be able to overcome. This is what's going to stop me in life"? A lot of times, underdogs and top dogs alike get knocked down in life. Many of us are unable to get back up and keep going, but a true underdog always gets back up as they know it is just another road block in their journey.

We knew that there was a possibility that this was the one that was going to stop us forever, and it terrified us. It knocked us down at the kneecaps. Cendant offered my dad to open any type of franchise business that he wanted, as long as it wasn't in the tax industry. They offered him all of the money he could imagine in order to open up locations in any other industry. My father graciously declined their offer as he wasn't done yet. His dream of being the number one tax company in the universe had not yet been fulfilled.

"I don't want to die with number two on my tombstone!" he said.

My father was in his late forties and had built a company that had over a thousand locations, over twenty thousand seasonal employees, and hundreds of thousands of customers. What about the dream he had? What about all the lives he had touched? What about all those underdogs on whom he had betted? Now it was all gone. What had happened to our dream? How could we be able to overcome this?

When things get tough in life, learn from my favorite lady ever: my grandmother on my dad's side. We call her Big Grandma. I love her for everything she's done for me. She is the sweetest lady that you can ever think of. She told me a long time ago, "Times can get tough. When things are knocking you down in life, think of one simple phrase: 'It could be worse.'" You may have gotten into a car accident, and been unable walk for a week or two, but many people lose their legs altogether. You may have been knocked down in life, like we were when we lost our company. It seemed like we would never be able to accomplish our ultimate goal in life of being the top dog in the tax industry. But my family still owned a significant portion of the company and had made tens of millions of dollars. We had our health and our family. There were certainly a lot of things that could have been worse.

Whatever is going wrong in your life right now, just think to yourself: "It could be worse." Sometimes we take a lesson for granted. Learn from my favorite lady: "It could be worse."

You can also take a page from my dad's book on how to get back up:

John: I've always been grateful, whereas I find 99 percent of Americans to be ungrateful. I think that being alive and healthy and getting to live in Virginia Beach makes you one of the perhaps two percent or three percent most fortunate people in the universe. How could you complain about anything?

I can remember a long time ago, when I was in second or third grade, I saw a short bus pull up and I just felt so sad for those kids. If I ever have a bad moment, a bad day, or a bad hour, I think about the people who are blind, deaf, or crippled. I've been blessed not only with the talents that I've been given in terms of my ability to grow businesses, lead people, and reach my dreams, but also with good health. You don't realize how important your health is until you get sick. The only time you really think about it is when you're sick because you take it for granted the rest of the time.

So many people take living in Virginia Beach, being healthy, and having healthy children for granted. Instead, people are always lamenting. I find that the people who complain and feel sorry for themselves spend so much time doing that that if they would just take that time and do something positive instead of sitting there complaining about something, then their life would be totally different. They would be winners instead of losers. The losers spend all of their time lamenting about what they don't have instead of doing something about it. I've virtually never had a bad day in the sense that I'm always grateful for all the blessings that I've received.

Chapter 8
True Underdogs

Let's talk about true underdogs: the entrepreneurs and small business owners that put it all on the line every single day, the people who actually create jobs that employ millions, the people who built this country. Unless you are an entrepreneur yourself, it's hard to know just how much work bleeds into life and life bleeds into work. Aside from the entrepreneur them self, the entrepreneur's spouse and children may be the one of the few groups of people that would really understand the hard work and sacrifice making your way entails.

When parents are self-employed and just starting to find their way, the children often don't go to many after school programs and clubs. Sure, you get to play sports and that kind of thing, but the children themselves often feel motivated to help their parents because they see that they can make a difference in the outcome of the way their life is lived. A child's help and involvement in the family business does not only contribute to a rock-solid parent-

child bond; it can also have an effect on what's for dinner –
whether the family eats steak and potatoes or oodles of
noodles on a particular night. Over time, children can make
a big difference in the whole outcome for your entire
family.

I recall that my mom had a special dish called "MBN" –
milk, butter, and noodles. When I was a kid growing up, I
didn't quite understand what "MBN Nights" meant. All I
knew was that it was a filling and tasty dish my mom
would whip up using milk, butter, and noodles. It doesn't
require a lot of ingredients and is incredibly simple to cook.
Allow me to eliminate any uncertainty for you; you cook
some noodles, and you put the noodles into warm milk and
butter. BAM! Not quite an Emeril dish, but it worked for
us. If you're feeling fancy, add a dash of salt and pepper to
it! Later in life, around my freshman year of college (go
figure), I realized that that particular dish is not only super
easy and fast but also super cheap.

The reason we would eat that way on different days and
nights was because it was a not-so-great week or a really
bad day for us. When your parents and family are self-
employed, everyone is a team together. Everyone has to do
it together. We won together. We lost together. There is no

"Mom goes to work," and you don't know what Mom does. Everyone is involved in the decisions of the business. We talk about it at the dinner table. It's a continuous conversation. It's their life. It's your life...it's our life. It is just what we do.

As part of the team, I was ready to jump into the family business wholeheartedly once we lost Jackson Hewitt. In the Jackson Hewitt days, I had grown up doing everything in my mom and dad's tax offices. I prepared tax returns, filed paperwork, answered the phone, and I was even "appointed" as the director of customer service. By the end of our journey with Jackson Hewitt, I had been in every job and played every role in the company because that was just what needed to be done. I remember when I was sixteen years old, and I would take phone calls from all around the country, from St. Louis, Chicago, or Miami. No one called to tell me how great their experience was; they were *all* very upset. I realized that since my last name is Hewitt, they would think that I owned the company, that I was 65 or 70 years old and that I could solve their problem with a simple wave of my magic wand. They seemed to think that if they yelled at me loud enough and kept me on the phone long enough, I would grant any wish they wanted. It got to the point where, for a short period of a few weeks or months, I started answering the phone as, "Danny Johnson"! It wasn't that I was afraid of dealing with these folks, but I cared about addressing their concerns, and I wasn't able to get far enough past the, "oh you're a Hewitt" reaction to understand what it was I could do to help!

I would travel all over the country with my parents when they visited Jackson Hewitt offices to help people expand and grow their businesses to compete as an underdog in their city. One time, in the early days, when I was only about twelve years old, we went to California, and we were visiting a Jackson Hewitt inside the Montgomery Ward. While we were there, my mom and dad suddenly couldn't find me. They started to panic as if they had lost me in the store. Eventually, they looked down the hall and saw me walking up with this business owner, a younger man who had opened up a small t-shirt shop inside the Montgomery Ward. I had taken him all around the Montgomery Ward, talking to him, showing him how, "You need to move your signs here, Sir. You need to put the shirts on this section. You need to hang another sign up over here to maximize your opportunity to be more visible, and you need to position your kiosk right in the front of the mall entrance." The reason I was doing this was because I had grown up knowing these things. I grew up watching my parents give this type of advice to so many underdogs just like this owner. The man was so excited that he actually asked my parents if he could hire me when I got older. The whole point of this story is to illustrate that when you grow up in a family that is building a business, it becomes a part of you and part of everything you do.

When you're a business owner, you are always looking for more ways to draw business into your store. You can't just sit down with the lights off, or even lights on, and wait for people to come in. When we started Jackson Hewitt back in the day, there was no such thing as cellphones, Internet, or GPS systems. You couldn't say to your phone, "Hey, find me the closest McDonalds." There was obviously no Facebook, LinkedIn, Twitter, or any of the different social media. None of these things that we take for granted today existed when we started Jackson Hewitt.

However, at the point of time where we had now arrived, some of those things were coming into existence. Technology was changing the world and life as we knew it. I remember my mom and dad talking about a book that would have a huge impact on my life. They loved how the author had new creative ways to advertise and grow businesses. The author's name was Jay Conrad Levinson. He wrote a book entitled *Guerrilla Marketing*. My mom and dad understood his vision of how, just by using your head and being a little bit more creative than everyone else, you could make a huge impact on your business and compete with companies who had significantly more finances to invest in marketing. Levinson said that Guerrilla Marketing wasn't taught in traditional marketing classes. It wasn't something that you could just pay for off the bookshelf. It was something that you had to religiously embrace.

I met Jay when we hired him to be the keynote speaker in one of our national conventions for Liberty Tax in the late nineties. He was a little bit older by now, but he still had spunk in his step. It was awesome to show him how my family had not only listened to his words but taken them to heart and used them to enable us to compete in the industry with such a huge competitor dominating the industry. Mr. Levinson believed in the underdogs and helped millions compete against industry giants just as we did. He is a legend, and his teachings will continue to help others in future years. Thanks for your pioneering, Jay.

During the Jackson Hewitt days, when I was fifteen years old, my mom and dad separated. My mom, who embodied the entrepreneurial spirit just as much as my dad, decided to purchase several stores in Norfolk and Virginia Beach that focused on offering shipping and copy services, as well as income tax preparation. I was in high school and made the choice to stay with my mom and help her grow her new business. I spent countless hours for the next few years helping out in her stores, cleaning toilets, marketing and operating our locations while she was busy in other aspects of the business. It was our life – day in and day out. We didn't get days off or much vacation. We worked with our business and served our clients.

My mom needed to make any type of revenue that she could. In a tax business, we typically only make money four months of the year. So my mom decided to make a program called "Copy, package, ship." It was a company that we split down the middle of our Jackson Hewitt offices. It provided extra revenue for our family. We did everything from notaries to faxes. We had PO boxes. We would ship packages out for people. I even remember helping my mom launch a pager program. Yeah, pagers were the big thing in the nineties to those of you who can remember that era. We did anything to generate extra income in the tax season and the off-season. My mom had to feed the family. It was our livelihood. I learned a lot from these younger years of my life.

It was about that time that I first wore a costume and began my journey down the path of being a full-time guerrilla marketer. I started dressing up on the side of the road on Virginia Beach Boulevard. It's probably one of the busiest roads in my hometown. I was dressed up as presents with a bow on my head and shipping packages such as FedEx and UPS. My mom would say, "Danny, wave at those cars. Let them know we're here. Let those people know we're inside and that we'll ship their packages for them." Life is all about choices, and fifty percent of the battle has always been and always will be simply letting people know what choices they have. All we had to do was let them know where we were and let them choose if they wanted to come in or not. While listening to my Walkman, I would dance in a costume for my mom's business and do whatever it took to let people know her business was there and that they could go in and support us. When the time came for someone to make a choice, at least they would know where we were.

Once our life, our dream, our vision was knocked out from under us with the loss of Jackson Hewitt, we wanted to continue in the business. However, in order to compete again, we had to create a new culture, behavior, and style in our new company. It couldn't be a regular old company. We would take the best things about the companies we had worked with and built in the past and combine them with the principles that we wished that companies from our past had been built on.

Also, if we were going to compete all over again, why wouldn't we want to work with the right people? With who would we want to work? Think about it. If you got to start all over, you would get to hand-select your team, coaches, and trainers, the people that you work with, the people you spend most of your time with. Then who would you pick? Who would you want to have on your team when you decide to walk into the ring as an underdog again? When you're competing, you get to choose your team all over. What are the things that matter to you about the team? What is most important?

We wanted to work with people who had values, morals, and ideas that were similar to our own. We wanted to work with people who we saw could get knocked down but still get back up. We wanted to work with winners. We knew that we were going to be in it for the long haul. It wasn't going to be easy. We knew it was going to take everything we had, and we knew that we needed a team who would give as much as we were prepared to give in order to achieve success.

Chapter 9
Perseverance Sets Underdogs Apart
From the Pack

In 1997, we opened Liberty Tax. Everyone told my dad
that he was crazy – again. They said there was no way he
would be able to do it – again. How could he compete in
this new age and this new world? How could he compete
against two top-dog companies? By this time, H&R Block
had nine thousand locations that were on the S&P 500. In
addition, they had brand name recognition, thousands of
employees, and millions of customers. They were one of
the largest companies in the world and had billions of
dollars in the bank; they were, in a word, humongous.
Jackson Hewitt, the name that we had built, now had two
thousand locations and our name on the front door. They
had worked with us for over fifteen years, and they knew
everything that we taught them. They had huge investors
backing them. They even the software that we had created
and developed year after year. How were we ever going to
compete?

We knew that if we were going to do it again, we had to jump in full force. We had to let everyone know that we were in town. We had to compete harder than we have ever competed before. We had all the odds against us. Was it even going to be possible? How were we going to do it all again?

There were less than ten people in our team when we started. We created our plan, our vision, and our dream once again. I was only nineteen years old at the time. I drove to Columbus, Ohio, and opened five offices there. My dad had a non-compete clause with his previous employer, so he couldn't compete in most places in the United States. Therefore, we also opened in Canada.

My dad had a good background in Canadian tax. He knew it and understood it from growing up in the tax business in the northern states. Consequently, we were able to get into the Canadian offices pretty quickly. We called up the largest competitor of H&R Block in Canada and asked them, "Hey, do you have a hundred offices? You've been competing against H&R Block for the past several years, but you aren't able to capture much market share from them. We had thousands of offices in the United States. Let's partner together. I want to bet on you, and you can bet on me." We combined companies to what you know today as Liberty Tax. They shared a similar vision and, most importantly, had similar ideas on what they wanted out of this venture.

Once Al Gore invented the Internet, life changed. The Internet changed the world as we know it today. If you want to know where the closest Walgreens is now, you can Google it or type it in your GPS. Information is at your fingertips. You can have whatever you want anytime you want it. People's attention today is taken by cellphones, social media, and Apps and games on your phones. Everyone wants you to pay attention to them. Everybody wants a moment of your life. They try to steal your attention as much as they can.

We knew that if we were going to do it all again, we had to get noticed. If we were going to do this, we couldn't just dangle our toes in the water, and we were aware of that. We had to jump all in with both feet. H&R Block was getting bigger and stronger than ever before. And to make the situation worse, H&R Block knew that we were a threat to deal with this time. When we opened Jackson-Hewitt, they didn't pay attention to us, but we had already shown them that we were not people that you should underestimate.

They knew that once we jumped into this ball game, into this competition one more time; we were going to be a threat to them from the day one.

There was also Jackson Hewitt, the company with our name on it. This company that my family had built with our blood, sweat, and tears was going to be another huge threat. Our friends and our family still worked there. Now there was also Turbo Tax on the Internet. We had no clue how the Internet was going to develop, but we knew that it wasn't going to be easy to compete with. We had so many things going against us, and we had to start all over from the ground up one more time. Starting over with no offices, less than ten employees, and no customers would in most people's mind be insane. But we still did it. That's what underdogs do; they compete even when all the odds are against them.

You ask my father, "Why did you start Liberty Tax instead of buying an island and just hanging out?" My dad had owned a percentage of Jackson Hewitt. You don't need to be a mathematician to figure out that he had made many millions of dollars himself when the company sold for 483 million dollars. It was enough to live comfortably for the rest of his life. What would you have done in that situation?

Would you have given up and retired? Would you enjoy life and travel the world? Would you start another business? What would you have done if that were you in your late forties with millions of dollars?

My dad said, "I don't want to die with the number '2' on my tombstone. I've already achieved that in life." My dad was so close to being number one. He had grown his company, Jackson Hewitt, from the ground up to a major competitor in the tax industry. He still wanted to pursue his dream, and this time we came to play ball. This time we came to win. He has been called a Serial Entrepreneur, and now you see why. Many things will get in our way along the journey, but nothing will stop us as we are true underdogs ready for battle.

Perhaps you know the feeling; it's that deep desire inside. It's a yearning to win where nothing will stop you. Nothing! It's what makes you jump out of bed instead of pushing the snooze button one more time. Every one of us has that deep desire inside. All you have to do is dig deep inside and pull it out. It keeps you up at night thinking about what else you can do. It gives you a goal or a dream. It makes you work harder and longer than you ever have done before. It gives you a feeling of, "I can do this. I'm going to do this. There's nothing that can stop me." You visualize the way it will look once you have accomplished your dream, your vision, and your goal. You can't imagine not being able to do it. You train until you can't train anymore. Then you train again because you have to win. You have to train more than everyone else to have a chance. Even with a slim to none chance, there is a chance if you practice, train, and work hard enough. Then just maybe you can win.

No matter what anyone tells you, if it isn't in line with your goal, your dream, and your vision, you won't even hear it. You won't listen to it. Your attention is on the win, on the end-result, the dream, and the goal. It drives you with everything that you have. Have you ever felt so strongly about something in your life? Have you ever had the deep, burning desire to jump all in to give it everything you have?

One of our employees at Liberty Tax, Michelle in Las Vegas, won the Employee appreciation contest. Her four-year degree is being paid for by Liberty Tax. Michelle had laser focus on getting her college degree before her children did. When she graduated high school, she wasn't able to afford college. However, it was a dream of hers from she was very young. After graduating from high school, getting right into work field, and eventually getting married and having children, she didn't think it was going to be an option for her. But Michelle had laser focus to get her college degree. She might not get her degree until her older son is in college. But Michelle knows that she is going to get it eventually. That's laser focus. Nothing and nobody will ever stop her. We took a gamble and betted on an underdog like Michelle. She had the desire deep inside – that feeling that you will win no matter what. She is an underdog. She is a winner.

Do you have that deep desire inside? Have you ever felt like an underdog and longed someone to bet on you? You know that you are a great bet. All you need is somebody to bet on you. Nothing is going to stop you. Nothing is going to get your way. You know that there will be bumps in the road. It's not going to be easy. People are going to tell you that you can't do it. It doesn't matter what will happen today, tomorrow, or the next day; you are going to win. You just know and feel that you are going to do it. I think you do. You are just like us. You are the ones that we want to bet on. Tell me about what drives you. Tell me about your dreams, your goals, your aspirations, and your visions.

I want to hear about them. Why should somebody bet on you? You already know why deep down inside. Is it time to let it out?

You have to believe in yourself. In order for anyone else to bet on you, you need to start by looking at what's inside of you. No one else is going to believe in you if you don't first believe in yourself. You have to believe deep down all the way to your core. You have to stay up late at night thinking about it. People want to believe in you just like you believe in yourself. They want to help you achieve your dream and your goals, anything that you want to do in life. Let them help you. You deserve it.

It isn't easy being an underdog. We all know. People are going to point their fingers. They're going to laugh at you. They're going to tell you that you can't do it. Don't listen. Block them out if it's not part of your goal, your vision, and your dreams. Believe in yourself first. Only then can others believe in you.

Here is my mom's advice in overcoming unforeseen speed bumps or road blocks:

Linda: I believe very strongly that God gets us to where we are supposed to be, not necessarily where we choose to be. My faith in God gets me through almost anything in life. I have faith that I am right where I'm supposed to be because that's where God has put me. It's not always where you think you should be and at the time you want, but He knows the plan a lot better than we do.

There are two ways for you to look at your circumstances. You can look at the woes and feel sorry for yourself because of what has happened to you, or you can look at things that happen to you as opportunities. I believe that you should look at things as an opportunity to make some change, regardless of what it is, whether it is in your life, physically, financially or emotionally. Consider those as opportunities rather than do like too many people who go around and say, "Oh, poor me." I'm not a "poor me" person.

This is some great advice from my mom as always. Mom, your life lessons have helped me become who I am. I am forever in your debt.

Chapter 10
Corner Performers

When we were getting ready to compete again, we had to choose a new name. Our name was on our last company, Jackson Hewitt, and it went with it, so we weren't able to use it again. Therefore, we had to start from scratch and decide on what name we were going to choose to compete again.

At the time, my dad went on a trip to Las Vegas. While he was there, he passed by a Liberty shopping center that had an imitation of the Statue of Liberty in the front. He saw the name and the Statue of Liberty, and said to himself, "Wow, that's something that people would remember. That is a sign of individuality and of freedom to be who you want to be." Consequently, we chose the name Liberty. We chose to be unique.

The Webster dictionary defines the word liberty as the power to act as one pleases. For years I've heard my dad talking about being different from his competitors. I'll let him elaborate a little on that in his words:

John: I'm driven to succeed. If you do things the way everyone else does, then you get what everyone else has. So you have to do things differently. Chuck Lovelace came to me ten years ago and said, "I had an epiphany last night. You teach us to think outside the box, and we think outside the box, but then we fall back in the box. I realized that you are never in the box." I drive for a solution. I look in places other people don't think of, and I do things that other people don't think of.

Liberty seemed like a name that every household could remember, and it was one that all of us could stand behind and be proud of. My last name is Hewitt, but I like "Liberty" better than Jackson Hewitt today, even though my name is on over six thousand locations worldwide right now.

Because we were the underdog, we decided to choose a name that we would always remember and be proud to stand behind. The name gave us a chance to be ourselves – to be who wanted and chose to be. We wanted to be the number one tax company in the universe. That was our goal the entire time. Our goal was to be a winner, and that's why we live every day like a winner. It is a choice we continuously have to make each and every moment we are alive in this world.

When we are kids, before school, at the ages of five and under, we play outside the lines, we draw outside the lines, and we color outside the lines. We get crazy. We have fun. We try not to follow any rules. We don't know the rules yet. But once we get into school, whether that's kindergarten or first grade, we're always told, "Hey, get back in line," "raise your hand," "speak when you're spoken to," "don't talk out of turn" and "don't act up." At the restaurant, we receive crayons and a piece of paper and are told to color within the lines. You're going to get in trouble when you do things that are out of the normal.

Our society trains us to work inside those lines to be normal. But what is normal? Who is normal? Show me somebody who you think is normal, and I'll show you the abnormality about them that makes them who they are! Everyone who is normal has something abnormal about them. People are designed to be different and should not shy away from their differences. Be proud of *you* and who you are. Our name "Liberty" stands for power to act as one pleases. Isn't that what all of us want? We want be ourselves – our own-selves, not the selves that we perceive others want us to be. We want to be individual people, and we want to be accepted as our individual selves.

We decided to bet on franchise owners versus company stores. In all industries, franchise owned stores beat stores run by company employees. It's a natural thing when the owner is involved to outperform the company-owned location. If the franchise opens at 9 am, and a client walks up and knocks to the door at 8:45, the owner is more likely to open the door and welcome the customer in than the employee of a large corporation. When the owners are just stockholders who are a part of the system and part of a bigger society, the employee is less likely to open that door. They're going to wave, shew the person off and say, "Hey, we don't open till 9 am. Come back when we open up." If you're the owner, you go above and beyond what the employees of the large national chains do because it is your livelihood.

John: You can find a very small percentage of employees who will act like owners, but most owners act like owners. Ownership is the key word. When you own a franchise, you act like an owner. You work harder, smarter, and you go the extra mile. On average, you're always going to do better than a company employee.

Linda: Also, local owners are not only accepted in their community, but they are also a part of that community. It's hard for people to go into another area and open a business. You have to have business partners to help you do that. The way to do that is to let them have a piece of the pie by franchising.

Chad: If you want to grow any business, identify the small percentage of employees that act like owners. They are the diamonds in the rough. And give them the opportunity to shine. They will not only help your bottom line but also help raise the bar of every employee with whom they work. This, in turn, will raise the bar of your entire business. The sooner you realize that the biggest asset any business has is the people that work there, the sooner you'll break the self-imposed barriers that keep small businesses small!

When we started franchising the Liberty brand, we chose local owners: people who wanted to compete against the big companies with their big paychecks. We chose people who put in their life savings, their 401K plans, their retirement plans. They invested in themselves. They invested their paychecks, their families' money, and loans to get to themselves into the business. We invested in those individuals because we could relate to them.

We quickly advanced to one of the fastest growing franchise companies in the world by partnering with thousands of individuals just like you and me. That was one of the best things we've ever done to succeed as the underdog. All we did was invest in underdogs, people just like you and me. People invested their life savings just for a shot at achieving their dream, a dream they spread in their towns and their communities. They began competing against bigger systems, bigger companies, bigger checks, and bigger bank accounts. They chose to become the underdog. Liberty Tax has loaned or invested hundreds of millions of dollars into people who have that burning desire to compete with us.

We believe in our people. At one point, we had five thousand employees dancing on street corners all over North America. People ask us all the time, "Why don't we see Liberty Tax in a national commercial, for example during the super bowl, when other large companies do that?" Why did we choose to employ five thousand people to dance in costumes on the side of the road instead of betting on one sixty-second Super Bowl commercial? We wanted to stimulate the economy for every underdog we bet on. When we would open a store, we could buy one radio commercial, or we could pay five people in that community to let everyone know that we were there to file taxes in this community. Besides, these days, most people can remember at least two corners where they have seen a corner performer dancing, waving, or spinning a sign. Can you remember two commercials from last year's Super Bowl?

We believe in the people stimulating the economy. That is why we employ hardworking individuals who are willing to work in the sleet and the snow, day in and day out – people like your mailman, who no matter what the weather is, always shows up. No matter if it rains, snows, or if it's windy outside, he's always there. People who need to pay their rent, their mortgages, and their water bills, and people who need money to put food on the table for their families, those were the people in whom we wanted to invest. When we invest in them, they invest in us. It is this principle that has helped the Liberty system grow faster than any other franchise in the tax industry and has garnered dozens of awards for us. As Chad said, "Your people are your number one asset."

We want to bet on the underdogs: the people who are willing to work hard and give it everything, everything that they have and are willing to do. By traveling in the U.S. and Canada and waving on almost every street corner myself, I've had opportunities to see all walks of life. We've employed people who were tall, short, big, small, old, young, men, women, and every nationality you could imagine. We have even employed handicapped and blind individuals. In Louisiana, we employed a blind lady to dance on the side of the road for us. She was one of our best wavers ever. The smile never left her face. Can you imagine how many obstacles she had to overcome just to be able to accept a job waving on a street corner? That's determination. We bet on people who choose to act as they please to act, people who are willing to stand out and be different, unique and individual. Are you willing to just be you?

You have a chance every moment to make someone's day better, or worse. What will you choose? All over the U.S. and Canada, you find people dancing on the street corners, waving at vehicles day in and day out in tax season. When I'm on a plane wearing a logo shirt, the first thing people ask me is, "Are you one of those guys dancing in the Statue of Liberty costume on the main street?" I always respond, "No. I am *the* guy dancing in the Statue of Liberty costume on the main street!" I learned that response from one of our greatest dancers ever, Jerron Dennis, better known as Worldwide. Thanks, Dennis, for showing me some sweet dance moves along the way.

Our company became known as the company that puts people on the side of the road to wave in business. Imitation is the sincerest form of flattery. Many other industries have tried to copy us but failed: Firehouse subs put firemen at the side of the road; Little Caesars have pizza sign shakers; Subway has guys dressed up as a sub; Chick-fil-a has a cow, and Ronald McDonalds waves for McDonalds. There are many characters out there from other businesses and other industries. Many other companies have tried to create thirty thousand brand ambassadors. Why were we able to do it? Why was Liberty able to create the thirty thousand ambassadors to one brand when others have tried and failed?

You have probably never imagined the length of the day of someone dancing on the side of the road or alongside the corner. Perhaps you never have thought about how every car that drives by reacts toward it. Many of our performers will see thirty thousand cars in an hour. People are waving, smiling, and dancing with us. At a brief moment, we get a chance to make an impact on their lives. It's only a moment, only a second. They may be driving 35, 45, sometimes even 55 miles an hour past us. Right then and there, we get a choice. We can make a difference in how their day is going to be. Many parents have said to us, "My children asked us to drive by the waving Liberty."

Every moment in your life, you get to choose. The choice is not "will we" be able to change someone's life today. It is "how will we" change their life today. Do you want to make someone happy? Do you want to make a difference in their life? How do you want to help that person?

One of my favorite quotes by Zig Ziglar is: "You will get all you want in life, once you help enough other people get what they want." Zig Ziglar is one of the most well-known authors and public speakers around. He has written dozens of books which have helped hundreds of thousands, if not millions, of people. The lessons from his book help people perform better in their lives and careers, and they also help them to be better people.

Here's the key to this quote: "once you help enough other people." It starts with helping others. It starts with giving. We were taught at an early age that, "You must give in order to receive." We have to give to others in life. Without giving, you cannot receive.

My pastor, Ray Buchanan, who presided at my wedding ceremony, is one of the great influences in my life. In 1998, he started a non-profit together with my father that they called "Stop Hunger Now." My dad donated 400,000 dollars of the first 500,000 dollars to launch the non-profit, and he sat on the Board of Directors as Chairman of the Board. Over the years, we have raised over sixty million dollars in hunger aid to help all over the world. We've sent food to over seventy countries. They focus on communities that have starvation concerns, in places like Haiti, Honduras, and South Africa. I have been to these places myself, and I've met some of the most amazing people you would ever meet there. People there are so amazed by the little things in life that we take for granted each and every day.

Once, I visited an orphanage in Cape Town, South Africa. There were about 22 children there. Every morning, they would pick out clothes from a shared supply. The clothes were used by everyone. They would wash the clothes at night, and then the next morning, whoever woke up first got the first pick of the clothes. However, they didn't care what clothes they got that day. They were happy for the chance to have clothes. It was the little things that made them happy. Ray had and still has a vision, dream, and plan for us to stop hunger in our lifetime. We're betting on Ray as an underdog – another chance, another person to change the world forever. Thanks for all you have done, Ray. We are on our way to a world without hunger just as you envisioned.

My friends Robbie and Brittany Bergquist founded "Cell Phones for Soldiers," and we've able to collect hundreds and thousands of cellphones to help soldiers call home. Currently, at most of our Liberty offices, you can drop off an old cellphone in a collection box in the waiting room. We turn those old cellphones into cash and purchase overseas calling cards. We then mail these calling cards overseas to help soldiers call home. Cell Phones for Soldiers has made a huge difference in many people's lives.

The founders, Robbie and Brittany Bergquist, didn't want our soldiers to be stuck with huge telephone bills from calling home. They're fighting for our country, risking their lives for our benefit. The least we could do is help them be able to call their loved ones. Again, we're betting on the underdog, the person who is overseas and wants to call home to their friends, family members, and maybe their spouse. These two people have helped our world become a better place. Thanks for all that you, the Bergquist family, does for our military men and women. I look forward to continuing our support with your dynamite organization.

After dancing on the street corner for hours, you begin to find who you are. Being on the street corners could be one of the most boring jobs in the world, or it could be the best job in the world. With every chance when you're on the side of the road, you get to make it or break it. You get to choose what you want to make of it – what you make of each and every moment you have.

A few years ago, I spent over a hundred days in Portland, Oregon, for tax season. It rained 95 out of those 100 days. Did that mean that we didn't go outside and wave business in? Did that mean that we didn't have to be happy in the street corners when we waved at people? No, if we were truly going to compete, we had to get out there and wave traffic into our stores. It didn't matter what obstacle was in our way; we had to overcome it if we want to win.

No matter what life throws at you, try to find the positive. Try to find happiness in everything you do. On those days when it rains, dance in the rain. When you feel yourself going into a negative state, when you have trouble finding happiness, when something hits you so hard, and you think you're not going to be able to overcome it, remember the words from my grandmother, "It could be worse."

Chapter 11
Just Hewitt

Many people start new adventures and endeavors by dipping their toes in the water just to test it. They want to feel how cold it is or how warm it is and see if they are going to get involved. Why do we do things halfheartedly? Why do we do them not all the way? Once you've researched the topic, weighed the risks, and determined that you're going to do it, you *must* jump in with both feet to submerge yourself if you really want to win. You have to give it everything you have. You can't hold back at all. While you are testing the water, somebody else is giving it their all, learning, training, practicing, and becoming better than you are. They're doing what it takes to win, and a halfhearted approach will be left in the dust every time.

Bruce Lee said, "I fear the man that has done one kick ten thousand times, not the man that has done ten thousand kicks one time." It is the practice that enables you to win.

When my son was wrestling for his high school team, he found out very quickly that the person who trains the most usually wins. Getting pinned most of his first matches as a new wrestler, he realized very quickly that he needed to train harder and longer in order to win. He would have to train more than the top competitors if he was ever going to get a chance to compete. If his competitor had trained two thousand hours and he had only trained five hundred hours, he would be sure to lose.

As he began to learn this valuable lesson, he started running after practice for endurance. He practiced moves after the normal school wrestling practices. He woke up early and practiced wrestling in his spare time when other people were just goofing off. If he didn't, he would continue to get pinned by people who were taking their dream seriously. Those who had that burning desire deep inside that drove them to wake up early and practice and stay up practicing late at night until they would crash, those were the ones who would win. The determination to go over and over again and do more than anyone else is what drove him, but the practice is what made him win.

Henry Ford said, "You can have anything you want, but you can't have everything." You have to establish a clear vision or goal early on. That will keep you focused on what you need to do day in and day out to win. It will paint the yellow brick road for you. It will allow you to paint the road of success that everyone will need to follow.

We've all been told by countless self-help gurus to write down our goals, and put them somewhere visible so that we can see them. But how many of us have them on our bathroom mirrors or dashboards of our vehicles? Why so few? We knew that we needed to share our vision with others to make it become more of a reality. How many people have you shared your vision with this month? Have you even written your goal down yet? *Do it now!* I mean, how badly do you want your goal? *Write it down!*

At Liberty Tax, we have a goal of being the largest tax company in the Universe by 2020! The goal has been set, written, and shared among everyone we know. We have been able to empower many individuals that have a similar vision in their hometowns. People just like you and me – people who have a dream and vision – are competing all over the Universe for this same goal. They are driven to make their dreams come true.

Too many of us surrender because we don't establish that clear vision early on in the process. We say that we have a dream, vision, or goal, but do we have a clear vision? Do we really have that clear path that we set for ourselves? Do we have that deep desire inside that makes us get up when it seems impossible – when everything is in front of us?

Take your dream, your vision, and your goal by the horns. This is your goal. Own it! This is your vision. See it! These are your life aspirations. Achieve them! They are yours, not anyone else's. Nobody is going to believe in you if you don't believe in yourself. No one is going to help you if you don't help yourself. Don't be afraid to fail. Name a single person who hit a home run at their first at bat. Name a single person who threw touchdown on the first down of their first game. Every failure gets you that much closer to success.

Raising four kids has made me realize that when you fail in something, you have two options. You can either be mad at yourself for failing and let that prevent you from trying something again or you can learn from your mistake and use that knowledge to reduce the chances of failing in your next attempt. For example, you may tell your child, "Don't put your hand on the stove. It is hot." If you're an unfortunate parent like myself, unfortunate enough to have one of your children put their hand on the stove top as I am, then you know that that will be the last time they'll ever do it. If they put their hand on the stove and it burned them, they will never put their hand on the stove again. But very rarely will a child not ever try to help in the kitchen again. My son learned very quickly that the stove was hot. He learned that the moment he touched it. The moment he failed, so to speak.

Failure helps us learn very quickly. Because failing involves first trying to do something, the lesson we learn is exponentially more valuable than lessons we learn from researching things before actually trying it. You will learn from your mistakes. It will make you a stronger competitor. Underdogs fail. Underdogs get knocked down. Underdogs do not win every time. But they get up again. They keep on fighting. They don't ever give up. They persevere.

One of my favorite underdog stories growing up is probably the favorite for many: the life of Rocky Balboa. He was a guy who nobody thought had a chance. He had lost his first seventy fights. The champion was so strong and big, and many people thought that he was unbeatable. Rocky's journey to winning was not an easy road. He had to train harder than he had ever trained before. In Rocky 4, when he beat the Russian, he eliminated all distractions by going deep into the country of Russia to focus on his goal, his dreams, his visions, his success and nobody else's. He had to do that if he was going to have any chance of winning. He had to focus on winning.

You need to focus on your path to victory. Eliminate the distractions in your life that do not align with your vision if you truly want to win. Put blockades and walls in front of them, so that you can focus on what's important to you.

"Just do it" is not enough if you want to win. Go above and beyond in your training and your practice. You have to work harder and more hours than anybody else. Remember, they're training too. They want to win just as much as you want to win. In order to win, you must commit fully, put it all on the line, jump in with both feet, and "Just Hewitt!"

It comes down to who wants to win more. Who gets up and tries again when they get knocked down. Get up earlier than your competition gets up. Stay up later than they stay up. The difference between a person who makes fifty thousand dollars and the person who makes 500,000 dollars is that the latter does it a little bit more than the former. This could be you too.

When a Liberty Tax office opens in a new city, everyone knows that they have come. The owner of the new office employs costume characters from the local community to dance, wave, and entertain the patrons of their city. We bet on the underdog, and we encourage them to bet on the underdogs in their town. The next time you see a dancing Statue of Liberty, wave or honk at them, for that person is an underdog competing against much larger top dogs right in your town.

In the Olympics, we watch many people miss the gold medal and get the silver or the bronze medal instead. Although they are amazing competitors and although it's a huge accomplishment to get the silver or the bronze, how many of them actually have a goal to finish second in the Olympics? They all want the first place. No one wants to be the second. They all trained to be beat everyone else. The individual who trained the most is the most committed, and the one who executed as they have practiced is the one most likely to win.

You have to train harder and longer than everyone else if you're going to succeed as an underdog. It is so much easier to quit and give up. It takes a lot more to stick with it. It isn't easy to work through your problems and the speed bumps life throws at you and get up again to ask for more. It isn't easy to get up when you're knocked down.

Getting knocked down could take the wind out of you. You can get broken bones, scrapes, and bruises. I know it won't be easy to get up many times. I know you still want to throw in the towel. I know that some days and some moments, it will feel like the whole world is against you and that there's no way to keep going.

Fortunately, the tax business is changing all the time. New forms, tax laws, and now even healthcare regulated by the IRS force us to stay on top of our game. It forces us continuously to train and better ourselves for the individuals we are helping. Every tax preparer at Liberty Tax has to pass a certification test of their knowledge. We have Beginner, Intermediate, and Advanced Tax Knowledge levels. Why? Because we know how important training is. We know we are going only to be as good as our weakest teammate, so we constantly train for battle.

Don't give up, period. Every time you get knocked down, you're getting that much closer to the win. If it was easy, would you even want to compete? Isn't it so much more fun to compete when there's a challenge and when you actually have to work hard at it? How do you feel when you work hard on something, and then you finally achieve that dream, that goal, that vision that you had? You feel like you're on top of the world and top of your game. Then you're number one. You feel like you've accomplished something in life. The reality is that you have. You have done the impossible. You've broken all odds. You've done what so many said that you had no chance at. Isn't this what being an underdog is all about? Every underdog strives to be the top dog, and every top dog was, at some point, an underdog.

Picture yourself in the winner circle. The better you visualize the end-result before you get started, the more likely it is to happen for you. Create that clear picture, that image, every detail you can about being in the winner circle in your mind. How many lives will help along your way to the top? How many people will you have changed for the better? Make your mark in the world because nobody else is going to do it for you. Believe in your vision. Believe in your goal. Believe that your aspirations and your dreams can come true. I believe anyone can do it, just like so many other underdogs in the past, as long as you set your mind to it. I believe in you! Do you believe in you?

The following is my dad's advice on being the underdog and competing against the top dog:

John: An extraordinary entrepreneur is a risk taker. You've got to be a huge risk taker. My biggest risks by far are with business – not with horses, sports, crafts, or anything like that. The biggest gamble is with business and starting a business.

After leaving Jackson Hewitt where they had three thousand offices, my name, and my system, we faced the eight hundred pound gorilla, H&R Block, which had nine thousand offices, as well as Jackson Hewitt. We said, "Oh yeah, we're going to be number one by 2020. We're going to compete with these two guys." With no offices, that's insane. That is an illogical, unrealistic goal.

However, I don't think that God put us on earth to be ordinary. He gave us gifts to do something with them. I believe one of the worst things you can do in God's eyes, which is proven by my favorite parable in the Bible, the parable of the talents, is to not use the talents that He has given you. I believe it's almost a requirement from God to do something to change the world and do it in a different way. Fighting those huge companies like H&R Block with all their advantages of a brand name, money, established offices, established customer base, and established tax preparers is the David and Goliath story. If David hadn't come out on the field with a different weapon, if he had the same sword, shield, and armor as Goliath, he'd be guy number 184 killed by Goliath. You have never heard of the story of Bob and Goliath or Daniel and Goliath. You only heard of the story of David and Goliath.

You have to do things differently. You have to think of unique strategies. The number one thing that separates long-term winners from the average is perseverance. You have to persevere because no one put on earth is sacred. Everyone faces adversity. Everyone has to overcome obstacles.

Vince Lombardi said it best: "Winning isn't everything; it is the only thing."

When Liberty Tax was founded in 1997, nobody believed that we could compete against our own name and companies with huge bank accounts, millions of customers, thousands of offices, and tens of thousands of employees! But we believed in ourselves deep down! We believed that over time and through perseverance, we could prevail as the top dog in the tax industry! That is why we stay our course, keep training, continue to bet on the underdogs, and believe that we can do it. We are determined that in 2020, we will reach our goal! Focus on your dreams and aspirations and maybe one day your dreams will become reality too!

Chapter 12
Betting on the Underdog

In my lifetime, I've never come across a single person who hasn't felt like they were an underdog at some point in their life. In fact, most people, regardless of their current standing in life, feel like an underdog.

Sometimes they have felt like all the odds were against them. They have felt like their competition was bigger, stronger, faster and more likely to win and that life itself was betting on somebody other than them. It's not the best feeling in the world. It becomes a struggle each and every day to get out of bed and a struggle each and every moment to keep fighting and to keep trying to compete when you're the underdog. I know what it's like to be considered the underdog. I know how it is to feel like the whole world is betting on the opposite team and feeling like everyone wants them to win and not you. Why are they betting on them and not on you and me?

What you have to ask yourself is how badly you want it. If you listen to the inspirational speaker Eric Thomas, he will explain to you how badly you need to want it to be successful. You have to want it more than anything else in life – more than you want to sleep, more than you want to party with friends, more than you want to go out to dinner, and more than you want to study. You have to need it. Need it like you need food, water, and air to live; only then will you truly gain the success you desire.

In one of Eric's most famous speeches, he talked about a young student who went to the beach to meet the money guru early in the morning, like 4 or 5 am. He talked about how the money guru walked the student into the water little by little, until the student was almost under water. Then the old man grabbed the student by the head and pushed his head underneath the water. The student began kicking and throwing punches, desperate for a single breath. Then the money guru said, "When you want to be successful as badly as you want a breath, then and only then will you able to make it happen for yourself."

Do you really want to be successful, or do you want to dip your toe into the water and achieve just enough to make it through the day? How badly do you want it? If you want it enough and are willing to do something about it, anything can happen. Successful people are willing to do what unsuccessful people are not. Are you willing to give up your sleep? Are you willing to give up your extracurricular activities, your play time, your fun time, and even your Sunday fun days? Are you tired of not being successful? Are you tired of everyone betting on your competition?

If you want to be the best, if you want to win, you're going to have to try harder than everyone else. It's as simple as that. You're going to have to work on your dreams, your vision, and your goal more than anyone else does. Even when it seems impossible, even when it seems all the odds are against you, even when nobody else believes that your dreams are possible, you have to believe it to achieve it.

Gordon: Preparation is very important. Winning is the end-result. Winning a fight, winning a baseball game, winning against a giant competitor is the end-result. Once you know the end-result, you have to go into preparation. Talented people like Celine Dion and Barbara Streisand, who are phenomenal singers, practice. They practice for hours. They're not born great. They have to practice so they can become great. Magic Johnson practices. Michael Jordan practices. LeBron James practices. That's preparation. Even the greater ones practice. So how much more preparation does the underdog have to do?

Sometimes you have to look for new pathways on how to win. You can't just say, "I want to win," or say "I believe I could win," and expect to do so. No. You have to follow through with the preparation. A part of that preparation is what you do mentally or physically, and also how you employ the knowledge and wisdom of others to overcome this particular objective you're trying to reach, this obstacle you're trying to get over. The wisdom of others can help you.

In the book *The Secret*, the author, Rhonda Byrne, talks about how you can do anything you want or be anything that you want. It is true that you can. You can do anything you want. You can be anything you want. There's nothing stopping you but you. Believe in yourself. Believe in your dreams. Believe in what you will be able to accomplish, and then you can do it. But nothing comes for free; in order to achieve, you must do. No one is going to do it for you. You will have to practice more than your competition and more than everyone else if you truly want to win.

Look deep inside yourself and make sure that this is the dream that you want to fight for and the dream that's driving you to win. Make sure that this is the dream you want. When everyone else doubts you, when your friends tell you that you're crazy and that you should find a new goal, and when your family tells you to not quit your day job because they don't believe you can do it, then you want to be sure that this is the dream you want to stick your neck out for. Believe in you, for it's the belief that will drive you through the tough times. You believing in yourself is one of the main keys to success. It is the start that you need to focus on before you will ever be able to seize your dream. Do you really believe in your dream? Do you have a feeling in your gut that drives you to get out of bed early, stay up late, and train when everyone else is giving up? It is this trait that you will need when everything else seems to be against you. As the founder of UBU, Ryan Duffield, says, "Be yourself, for you are the best at it."

Be ready to fail. Expect to fail. Failures are a fact of life for all competitors. Welcome your failures with open arms. Understand that when you fail, it is the fastest way for you to learn. You are so much closer to a win when you fail. Everyone is going to fall. Only winners are going to get back up. Get ready to pick yourself up to come closer to your goal. This is your vision! Own it. Don't be afraid to fail, welcome it.

Don't be scared to be knocked down. Don't be frightened to get knocked over. It is going to happen to each of us. Believe in your vision, and you will survive. Believe in yourself, and you will make it. Remember what my grandma said when the wind knocks down on you, "It could be worse." Remember that others have it harder than you and that God will never give you something you can't handle. Do not take the easy road and give up on your dreams, your vision, and your goals. Stick to the more difficult but extremely rewarding road. Stick to the game plan that you made when you entered the ring originally, but be prepared to let it evolve and adjust once the game has started. The road to the top is never straight. It winds this way and that and ebbs and flows like the waves in the ocean.

When times get so tough that you want to quit, take a moment to look deep inside yourself, and make sure you believe in you and believe in what you're competing for. Take the time to reflect on your beliefs when it seems as if the world is crashing down on you. When you truly believe in yourself and what you are doing, nothing can hold you down. No matter what happens, when you believe in yourself, you will get back up, and you can continue competing, even when it feels like there is no other option.

Don't want to take on the world by yourself? You're not alone. You don't have to. Together we can achieve anything. Tell me your underdog story. I want to hear your story. I want to hear what drives you; what motivates you? What inspires you? What makes you work harder than anyone else? What makes you stay up late and wake up early? What's that deep yearning inside your belly? Why should anyone bet on you? Why do you feel like the odds are against you? Why do you believe you're going to win? What is it that makes you feel like you're going to win? Why should I bet on your underdog story?

I know that you feel alone at times and feel like nobody wants you to win. I know I do, so I understand that feeling. I want the underdog to win. Betting on the underdogs in life is the most rewarding. Be different. Be unique and find underdogs on whom you can bet. Help the people who want help, the people who would be so grateful that you took the time to listen to them and help them. Bet on the people who truly want to be helped and are willing to put the time into the preparation to become the Top Dog. Bet on those who are yearning to be helped and desire that help, the people who are going against all the odds to win when everything looks like they can't win. They are still fighting and competing.

You're not alone. You're not the only one who believes in you or believes in what you do. Tell your vision to as many people as possible. Share your dreams, your visions, and your goals so that others can help you and join you in the race of the underdog. As you share your vision with others, it becomes more of a reality for yourself. You'll never know when someone will offer to stick their neck out to help you achieve your goals. You'll never know when someone believes the same thing you do until you tell them. Tell everyone. Tell as many people as possible. The more people you tell, the more likely it is that your dream will come true.

No matter if you win or lose in the competition, you'll always win if you sign up to compete. By competing as an underdog, you give others hope when it seems as if there is no hope. You allow others the chance to compete as an underdog alongside you. Everyone likes a great underdog story. It motivates and inspires us. I want to hear your story.

Although it is great to be the top dog at times, I *choose* every time to be the underdog. It is so much fun to win when everyone thinks you can't. Once you have that feeling, you will never quit. In life, you'll always find a higher peak to conquer just over the next hill. The lessons you'll learn by just trying will carry you to new places, new levels, new aspirations in life. It will help you achieve what nobody else thought possible. That moment when you finally beat the top dog – that split second when you have won and thereby beaten all odds and done what everyone said was impossible – is indescribable. That feeling makes you so proud of what you've been working so hard and so long for. You'll look back and say, "it was all worth it!"

Are you ready to compete? Are you ready to step into the ring with the top dogs? It will probably be the hardest thing that you have ever done in your life. You're going to get the wind knocked out of you. It's not going to be easy. People are going to tell you that you can't do it. Your close friends and family might tell you there is no way you can do it. Believe in yourself. Believe in your passion. Believe in your vision. Stay true to your vision.

You have just as much chance to win as anyone does. You can compete and win against anyone and anything you truly put your mind to. I'm betting on you.

Bill Gates once said: "The outside perception and inside perception of Microsoft are so different. The view of Microsoft inside Microsoft is always an underdog thing."

About the Author

Influential, infectious and passionate—Danny Hewitt is a sought-after motivational speaker for both small businesses and global corporations and brings to the table a great deal of expertise in guerrilla marketing and entrepreneurship.

Featured in the October 2009 issue of Entrepreneur Magazine, Hewitt is a successful business executive and the visionary behind several franchise ventures. Some of his endeavors include cofounding Liberty Tax Service in 1997 (where he currently acts as vice president of guerrilla marketing), along with establishing the Virginia Beach franchise of AArrow Advertising in 2009.

Hewitt understands the essential elements of owning and operating a business. Since co-creating Liberty Tax Service, he has worked in various capacities as a tax preparer, troubleshooter, store manager, franchisee, area developer and corporate executive. Hewitt has helped the company sell more than 4,000 franchises, prepare millions of tax returns and increase system-wide revenue to $100 million.

Beyond his entrepreneurial vision, Hewitt acts as a public speaker, team leader and as a business strategist/consultant. He brings a powerful message of change through the use of social media and guerrilla marketing tactics. He often speaks to corporate audiences about the viral forces that dramatically impact business practices and provides insight into fueling the development of growth strategies. Hewitt also works hard to inform business owners, chief executives, marketers and students on how to drive sales upward by utilizing innovative methods that turn time, energy and imagination into profitable results.

Some notable companies he has worked with to increase revenue and create interest and demand include Sears, Pizza Hut, Walmart, Ashley Furniture and many more. Additionally, he makes it a point to serve the community as an active volunteer for Talk About Curing Autism (TACA), Stop Hunger Now and Cell Phones for Soldiers.

As a consultant, Hewitt offers personalized attention and delivers impactful strategy, direction and content. He uses his extensive knowledge of leadership, franchising and grassroots marketing to develop action plans that propel companies to new levels of success.

Searching for Underdogs

I am very interested in hearing about your underdog story and how I can help. We are looking for companies with a strong core and desire to grow their business exponentially. If you believe your company is a good fit to compete nationwide or even globally then please contact me. Visit my website at www.howwehewitt.com to see if your company qualifies for me and my team's help. We are looking to help underdogs become top dogs in their industry. You could be the next Top Dog!!!

Thank you,

Just Danny